They Haven't Made An Ax That Can Chop Down A Dream

"Five Keys To Reinvention"

To Xavier
Let the thing that hurt you the most and use it as fuel that ignites the full potential that's lock inside of you
Lancelot Theobald

By

Lancelot E. Theobald, Jr.

Copyright © 2023 Lancelot E. Theobald, Jr.

All rights reserved. No part of this book may be reproduced or transmitted in any form or by any means, electronic or mechanical, including photocopying and recording, or by any information storage and retrieval system, without permission in writing from the publisher.

Published by: Books for Athlete www.BooksForAthletes.com

Dedication

This book is dedicated to my parents, who nurtured and guided me to be the person I am today. They instilled in me values, commitment, and a love for family. To my sister, who has always been, since we were kids, my number one supporter and advocate. To all my coaches and teachers, who have encouraged and helped me along the way, big and small, toward becoming the best I could possibly be. To my strong, positive male uncle role models, who simply, by example, showed me how to be a successful black man in America. To my uncles, Carl Theobald and Sam Belnavis, may they rest in peace, knowing you instilled in me everything I needed, just by being you. To my uncle Ted Holman, who is a living example of what it means to have an ardent lifelong commitment to a hobby that you love. To Karen Ferby-Guy who with no hesitation whatsoever became my eyes and ears when I needed it most. To Ray Smith, Richard Willis Jr., Tony Marlboro, Melanie Smith, Regina Gill, Ted Levy, Fred Sciaretta, sister Aimee Conan, and Brooke Schoenfeld, thanks for introducing me to new possibilities; and lastly, to my wife who has allowed me to be myself fully, with no apologies needed, but always making it clear she's got my back 100%. I love you.!!!!!!!

Family is Everything

5 Keys To Reinvention

1. Being comfortable in your own skin, know your worth, know you are worthy of anything your mind can conceive, you can achieve.

2. Surround yourself with people that have done what you're trying to do before and those that support and encourage you.

3. Educate yourself fully on whatever it is you are trying to do.

4. Be willing to put that work in, do whatever it takes, and however, no matter how long it takes to get what you want.

5. You have to, in your heart, believe that you can achieve.

Contents

Dedication: 3

5 Keys To Reinvention 4

Contents 7

Intoduction 7

Chapter 1: Near Tragedy Into Triumph 11

Chapter 2: Years when I went from a boy to a man 28

Chapter 3: Transition To Europe 53

Chapter 4: Testing The Grounds Of Entrepreneurship 77

Chapter 5: Introduction Into The Entertainment Business 95

Chapter 6: The Four-Year Dance Intensive 115

Chapter 7: Creation Of "T3 Technique" (The Theobald Tap Technique) 145

Chapter 8: Doing God's Work "Philanthropy" 163

Chapter 9: Creation Of The Trademark Fitness Programs 192

Chapter 10: Love-Hate Relationship, That Is Teaching 217

Conclusion 239

About The Author 241

Testimonials 244

Introduction

THis story is about a young man who, in one year, will go through five nearly tragic instances, which would propel him on a journey through life to discover his purpose in the pursuit of happiness. Happiness for each individual is different. One size and shape doesn't fit all, but for him, it had many sizes, many shapes, and many forms.

What he discovered through this journey called life is that happiness starts within. It starts with you being comfortable in your own skin. Being unique and living your truth will set you on a path to discovery of what God truly had in store for you. Come take a ride through this incredible journey and learn the five keys of reinvention, spiritual awareness, and ultimate success.

Follow his journey through life to see how he began to tap into his potential by following these five keys to unlocking the door to the discovery of happiness through self-reinvention. Take your negatives, turn them into your positives. Take the things that hurt you the most and use them as fuel that ignites the full potential that is locked inside of you. When you tap into your true potential, you will find the diversity inside of you that will open your heart to love, happiness, and ultimate success.

Chapter 1

Near Tragedy Into Triumph

MY senior year at Holy Cross High School would change my thought process, thinking, and trajectory in life for the rest of my existence, because of four specific incidents that happened within a year: a plane crash, train accident, car accident, and a near drowning, while witnessing a friend of mine drown right in front of me.

I got into a plane crash while visiting a college that was offering me a full scholarship. I'd actually hung out the night before traveling and was booked to fly on a private airline. I was exhausted, which wound up being a blessing. I recall getting to the airport and having to take a bus to the plane.

It was a small plane, and I remember being nervous and not really wanting to go. The other schools had flown me up on commercial airlines in the past, and I wasn't used to small private planes. While on the way up to Maine, due to obsessively cold weather in February, the windshield of the plane developed ice on it. The pilot turned on the de-icing fluid which caused a fire in the cockpit. Suddenly the front of the plane is on fire. I had been sleeping and woke up because there was smoke on the plane and people were screaming. I cleared my eyes and tried to focus, while the plane felt as though it was descending rapidly. I looked around, and there seemed to be a fire happening in the cockpit. There was smoke in the passenger area, the pilot's leg looked like it was on fire, and people were screaming and yelling. I said to myself; this has got to be a dream and went back to sleep. Right before I did that, there was a nine-year-old little girl sitting next to me who was traveling by herself. I distinctly remember her name being Sophie, her mom had asked me to look out for her. She was hysterically crying, and I grabbed hold of her, held on to her tight, and said, "Everything is going to be alright." I closed my eyes and went back to sleep. The next thing I knew, they were pulling me out of the plane. We had crashed into the frozen Scituate reservoir in Rhode Island. People died, but the little girl and I survived… yeah, we survived a plane crash. I never saw her again but have often thought about her over the years.

Once we tracked across the frozen reservoir, we were met by police, the fire department and the ambulance. We were brought to the nearest hospital in Rhode Island, where I was laid up in the hospital for a week. They had to make sure there were no fractures, or internal damage… I had broken my third metatarsal in my foot and had a knee injury, all things which would heal 100%.

Right after that, a few months later, I got into an accident while riding on a train coming home from Manhattan. The train derailed underground, moving fast and rocking back and forth. The lights were flickering on and off, which was normal for the train; all of a sudden, you heard a loud bang, and the train came to a screeching halt. The passengers, including myself, got thrown to the ground. You could hear these loud popping sounds, and when I looked out the train window, it was like the Fourth of July fireworks inside the tunnel. Suddenly, smoke began to fill the tunnel. I had never been in a situation where a train actually derailed, but I actually felt calm and unafraid. Immediately, I jumped into action, doing what I could to help the situation. I remember breaking the door window so that we were not trapped in that one car; we were able to at least move to the other train cars. As the smoke began to fill up inside the train, you could see the panic in people's eyes. Throughout this ordeal, I was completely calm, and within minutes, we had firefighters rescue us. They had to come down into the tunnel through one of the grates you see on the street. I had walked over these grates my entire life and never knew what they were for, but now I know, and thanked God for those grates. They rescued us one by one, through those grates—it was one hell of an adventure...

Shortly after that, I got into a car crash on graduation day, while on the way to my High School graduation. I forgot the tassels for my hat. I was with my girlfriend at the time, and we turned around to go back. I was rushing, not paying attention, had the radio station on—jamming. It was a beautiful day in May, and I was about to graduate. I went through a light without looking to my right, and all of a sudden, I heard my girlfriend say, "Lance!" before she could get the rest of her words out, pow!! We got into a head-on collision with another car. In my mind, I was like, "Did I just get into another damn accident?" Thank God I was driving around in a car my grandfather gave me back in the day. It was a dodge dart; I think those cars were made out of steel back then, because although the car was totaled, we didn't sustain any life-threatening injuries. Cops came and wanted to take us to the hospital, but I told my dad I needed to get to this graduation. I had worked too hard for this to let a head-on collision get in the way. Thank goodness, we were able to make it to the graduation. It started to become evident to me that God had his hand on my shoulder; but this next incident of the "tragic four," totally convinced me God had plans for me.

After the plane crash in February, the train accident in March, the car crash in May, I almost drowned in August and a friend of mine drowned right in front of me at Rockaway Beach. I will never forget my mom, who was just hysterical and looked to God when she wailed, "What did I do wrong that all this karma would come back on me—on my child?" that's when I looked at her and said, "Mom, what did you do wrong? What did you do right? I am still here. I am still standing. I have nine lives." From that day on, I felt I was this gift from God, and there began a mind shift. There are always two ways of looking at things. You can look at things positively, and you can look at things negatively.

I began to evolve to an eternal optimist. I felt that I was this gift from God here on this journey called life, to do something big, and to do something special. I began to, and still, approach life from the perspective that I have things that God wants me to do. Special things. I changed my complete outlook on life, due to those four tragedies, the "Tragic Four." Many people have unfortunate, or even catastrophic pasts. Many people survive various forms/levels of abuse, whether mental, physical, substance, etc., but there are two ways to look at that. You can look at it from a negative perspective; *why did this happen to me? I can't do it because…* or you can look at it as *I survived this, and I'm here for a purpose. I'm here to get things done.* The latter frame of mind is the way I approach life. Not to say it's an easy thing to do, but it can be done.

So, this chapter is basically about how these situations in my life allowed me to believe that I can achieve anything I want, because God has put me on this earth to do his work. It all comes from the simple fact that these "tragic four" instances changed my entire mindset. It's about mindset. I firmly believe that if I could change my mindset, anyone can; because I then began to internalize the mantra that I am worthy of all I set out to do; and with subsequent effort and work, I could achieve it.

One of the other crazy instances that changed my mindset was the summer of my senior year, after getting in the plane crash, the car crash, and the train accident, but before the drowning incident. I had gotten a job at an airline working with baggage. That's right, at an airline, and it was at the same airport that I flew out of when I got into the plane crash; see how ironic that is? I worked for the airline as a luggage handler; and one of the things we had to do was take the bags on and off the plane. We were taught to drive the baggage carts, which would take the bags on and off the plane; I'd just started learning how to drive a manual transmission. I didn't know how to drive a manual stick shift before this, which will be a very important part of the story in a moment. It took me a little while to get comfortable driving a stick shift, but after a while I got used to it, or so I thought.

I started driving these carts, made out of pure steel; they are heavy. If you ever really touch a plane, it feels like hard aluminum. It definitely does not feel like steel. I don't know exactly what the material is, but it feels like hard aluminum. One evening, they had parked the plane, a DC-9, at the airplane hangar. I was bringing food to be placed on the plane for the next day's takeoff. I arrived and dropped off whatever I had to drop off. I parked the baggage cart right behind the wing. Now, DC-9 wings are very low to the ground.

That day, as I sat in the baggage cart, I was putting it into reverse—unsuccessfully. Occasionally, the carts tended to jerk forward, or backward, depending on which way you were going, possibly because I had just learned how to drive a stick shift. At the end of the night, it was the last thing I had to do, before getting off work. It was Friday night, and I just got paid!!!! So, I got in the cart, and I put the gear in what I thought was 'reverse.' I turned around and looked back, and then lifted my foot off the clutch.

Instead of jerking and moving backward, the steel cart jerked and burst forward. I was trying to put the cart in reverse, because it was at the back of the wing, which was pretty low to the ground. As I was looking back, the cart jerked forward, and my foot flew off the brake. I couldn't control the cart as it drove right through the wing. It opened it up like a freaking can opener. Now you have to remember the carts are made out of pure steel, while these planes, which are dynamic and beautiful, are made of a lighter material. When I realized what had just happened, I panicked at the big piece of gaping hanging hard aluminum coming towards me, so I dipped to the side; and I was simultaneously grateful it missed my head by inches.

My family had just moved to Long Island from Brooklyn; my parents had bought this beautiful house. The first thing I thought about was either I was going to jail, or they were going to make us pay for this damage. I didn't know anything about insurance. You got to remember, I'm coming straight out of my senior year of high school, and I was frantic. I hopped in the cart, drove it back and parked it, signed out, and went home without saying a word. I was just nervous as all hell. My parents said they knew something was wrong, because usually, as soon as I get home, one of the first things I do is go to the kitchen to see what's in the refrigerator. They said I went upstairs to my room as soon as I came in, and they could hear me pacing back and forth.

They asked me, "What's the matter?" but, I said "Nothing." However, when your parents know you, they really know you, and they knew something was wrong. I was off for the weekend and was terrified about what was going to happen. I worried whether the cops were going to call the house, wondering how long would it take the job to find out it was me, and if I was going straight to jail. I figured that if they found out, I was surely going to jail. Nothing happened during the weekend, and I went back on Monday. As soon as I got to work, there was only talk of the airplane. They thought it was sabotage. They thought some Russians had come in and deliberately damaged the plane. If someone hadn't noticed the big hole in the wing and the plane took off, that could have been a cataclysmic situation, which I never even thought about.

So, they started doing interviews to figure out what happened, interviewing all the people that were around on Friday during that evening shift. They didn't know exactly when it happened, so I guess they must've interviewed me along with all the employees from Friday to Saturday morning, trying to piece together what happened. At that point, I was actually very calm. After about 15 minutes, they let me go, and I went back to work. Yet, there's a thing called your conscience, which is the number one thing you can't have if you're going to create an alternate truth. I was sweating, couldn't think, and could hardly work.

It took me about an hour before I returned to the office. I was taking a chance because I just knew I could be going to jail. Or my parents were going to have to pay for it, but I went in, and it was almost like I went in with my hands behind my back and said: "You can take me." I just couldn't deal with the guilt of knowing that I had lied, so I said, "Listen, I have to be honest with you. I did it, and this is what happened. I thought the cart was in reverse and it was in forward; it jerked my foot off the brake and tore a hole in the plane, and I'm very sorry."

I was saying to myself, "Please, God, don't let them arrest me." suddenly they said, "Thank you very much for your honesty. We've decided we're going to terminate you." not realizing what they meant, I asked, "When do I come back?" I had never heard of the term terminate before; I thought that's another word for suspension. They looked in my face and said, "Son, you're fired." in my mind, I was like, "Oh, okay, I'm good with that." This situation taught me that it's better to tell the truth in situations like this immediately because the truth will come to the light anyway. This was a lesson that I had learned that would be useful in years to come.

Soon afterwards, my dad arranged a meeting with management just to make sure the firing wouldn't be on my record. That's when they told him that they had insurance. They then asked my dad, "Was this your son's first job?" my father said, "No, he's worked before. Why?" And they replied, "He's a good kid, but he's very playful." One of the other responsibilities was to direct the plane to the gate after it landed. I would be out there with those glow sticks directing the plane while (at the same time) moon walking, dancing and waving at the pilots and passengers that were on the plane. Management did assure my dad it wouldn't be put on my record. A crazy experience, although I wouldn't put in the same category with the "Tragic Four", but it was another situation helping to shift my mind set. Upon reflection, it was just one more thing for me to realize that God had his hand on my shoulder. That year changed my whole perspective and trajectory in life. From that point on, like I said before, I believe I was this gift, and God was sending me on this incredible journey.

In the last experience of the "Tragic Four," I'd be remiss not to mention that we did lose a friend of mine that day. May he continue to rest in peace; his name is Jerry.

That crazy day went down like this: it was my uncle, his girlfriend at the time Veronica, my two cousins, Eric and Paul my best friend from Brooklyn, Jimmy, Jerry and me. We went to Rockaway Beach because someone suggested that we head out to go swimming. It was already around

6:00 pm, but we all said what the heck, jumped into our cars, and headed to Brooklyn. We did notice that no lifeguards were on duty. We didn't think anything of it, so we took our clothes off and jumped into the water. We had a blast; the water was nasty looking. You couldn't see your hands in front of you, but the waves were crazy and just crashing down on us. We were just having an awesome time enjoying ourselves. What we didn't know, as we romped around in the water, was the strength of that evening's undertow, which is why they suggest people do not swim. We noticed there was nobody there, and we figured that was our opportunity to get out there and have a good time without people being around. While we're out there, and the waves are crashing, and it was a terrific time—until it wasn't. All of a sudden, one person yelled, "I can't touch the bottom." and that set off a panic. I'm a lifeguard; but I'm a lifeguard in the pool, which is very different compared to a lifeguard in the ocean, as I came to find out. So, everyone started to panic, because the waves started getting really aggressive, and something was pulling us away from the shore... The first thing I see is my Uncle Brian looking like he was levitating and moonwalking on top of the water. He was literally running on top of the water and was able to get out. My man, Jimmy looked like he was levitating also, and running on top of the water—he got out. Then there was Jerry, Paul and myself. Jerry, who was in front of us, and my cousin, Paul, who was on my right side, were further out. At that moment, I wasn't panicking, because I was treading water.

Paul yelled out, "I can't touch my feet to the bottom!" So, what I did was dive underneath the water, then I looked to see how far he was from the bottom. It was so cloudy and murky, I could hardly see; however, I did notice he was only about three or four inches from the bottom. But the undertow continued to pull us out, and then the big waves were crashing us from the back, wrenching us further out from the shore, as we became more unhinged. Now, Jerry, who was in front of us, completely panicked and stopped fighting. And, before you knew it, he had whizzed past us like he was on a skateboard. Within what seemed like seconds, he was much further out than we were. As I'm watching this, I have my cousin who's like, "Yo! Help me, Cuz!"

What do I do? I used the maneuver that I learned in the pool, which can be quite different from being in the ocean. I grabbed him from the back, then I put my arm over his shoulder underneath his armpit, and I began to swim backward toward land. Suddenly, more waves crashed on top of us, and he panics, jumping on top of me. The maneuver I learned, is to submerge the person underneath the water to disorient them, then you hit them, which many times will force them to release the grip that they have on you because literally, he's on top of my neck, pulling me down with him. So, that's what I did. I went underneath the water; I hit him, then he released his grip. He didn't mean to do it, but he was hysterical. I was able to get from underneath him. At this point, my cousin and I are now fighting for our lives, literally. I'm a lifeguard and in great shape, but I'm swimming up against the undertow, which was winning. In hindsight, you're supposed to swim parallel to the shore, until you get out of the undertow. I didn't know that at the time. As I was swimming towards the shore, it was pulling me further out, I was exhausted, but still swimming, still fighting for my life.

Again, God was with me, because as I'm swimming, I'm getting weaker, I can hardly lift my arms out the water, but I'm still fighting. All of a sudden, I realized that I could stand up. By this point, I'm thoroughly exhausted… I had enough strength and fortitude to continue to fight, to get my body back onto the shore. God had just miraculously stopped the undertow. By this time, Jerry was a quarter of a mile out, and they say his arm went up, you could faintly hear, "Help, help, help!" Then his arm went down, and he just disappeared.

As all this is happening, my other cousin was still out there, fighting for his life. He would say, "Help, help!" And all of a sudden, he would just stop; it looked like he was drowning. But what he was doing was the dead man's float. He was holding his breath, conserving energy, because he wanted to live in the worst way. Every time he would stop yelling, I was like, "Oh no, now what am I going to tell my aunt? She is going to be pissed off." "What do you mean he died? You didn't die with him?" you know what I'm saying?

I didn't know what I was going to do. I'm desperately calling his name, "Paul, Paul!!!", then, all of a sudden, his head pops out the water again. "Help! help!" He's screaming, and I'm trying to muster up enough energy to go back out there to help him. Now, I see some people watching what's going on, and they're looking at me, and I'm looking at them, and I'm trying to get enough energy, and he's screaming, "Help! help!" Then, I notice that he is at a point now where the undertow has stopped. Although the waves are crashing him from the back, the water in front of him is a little more than waist high. Despite his horror in the moment, he can actually stand up. But he didn't even realize he was standing up, because he was so exhausted, and the waves were still hitting him from the back. So, another person and I ran out there, and I grabbed him; I said, "Cuz, you can stand up. You can stand up."

He grabs hold of me, and I'm like, "Oh god. Thank God, I don't have to tell my aunt her son died." we pulled him back to shore, and the first thing he says is, "What about Jerry? We got to get Jerry." I looked at him and said, "Cuz, he's gone, man. He's gone." the next thing we know, lifeguards appeared out of nowhere and started searching for Jerry, and they started diving and swimming underneath the water. I didn't know how they were going to find him in this big ocean, because you can't see what's in front of you." after a while, the lifeguards gave up.

About 45 minutes later, as we're getting ready to leave, somebody yells out, "Yo! Somebody else drowned!" This is about two beaches over. We hauled ass over there; they're doing mouth to mouth resuscitation. Now we're looking, and my inner thoughts are, "Wow, that's another black guy who drowned, because that's not Jerry." then, somebody said, "That is Jerry. That's his bathing suit." he had swallowed so much water, I couldn't even recognize him... I didn't even know that was him. They were giving him mouth to mouth, and as the water was coming out of his body, you see his hands moving and I thought, "Oh my god, maybe he's alive". After about

15 minutes of giving mouth to mouth resuscitation, and pumping his chest, they said he's gone, and we had lost our boy. The police made the call to his parents and never said who drowned. They just said, "There's been an accident at rockaway beach; come to the beach."

My mother was completely livid at that point. It's like she had gone through all these different disasters… a plane crash, car crash, train crash, now, he possibly drowned; in addition, my uncle, her little brother, as well as my two cousins are with him. What did I do wrong, God, for all this bad karma to come on me and my child? She was hysterical and thank God most of us survived. Jerry's mom arrived, and it was heartbreaking to hear her say, "Her baby was gone." Jerry's mother packed up and moved away after the funeral, and I never saw, or heard from her again. I often wondered how she was doing. That was a life-altering experience for me. After the year, of the tragic four, I just knew that I was a gift from God because these experiences were off the hook.

They Haven't Made An AX That Can Chop Down A Dream

They Haven't Made An AX That Can Chop Down A Dream

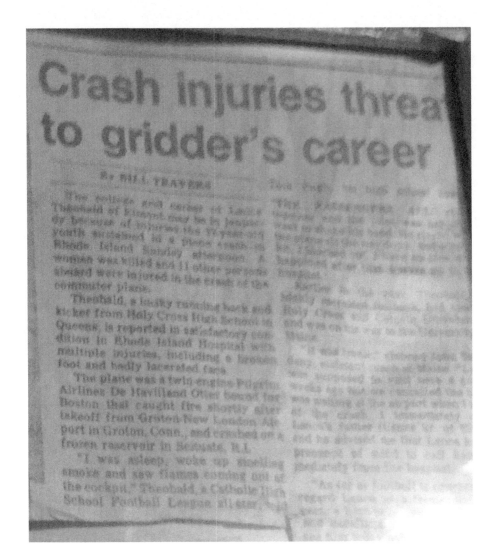

They Haven't Made An AX That Can Chop Down A Dream

Chapter 2:

After getting into the plane crash, I received letters from the other schools that offered me scholarships stating that they were rescinding their offer. Understandably, it was out in the news that I was involved in a plane crash and was now damaged goods. The University of Maine maintained its offer, so I decided to accept a full scholarship to the University of Maine.

Now, I'll never forget when I left that summer to go to football camp in Maine, and I remember leaving my house, very clearly and distinctly crying in every room, because I was leaving the nest. I was a confident, fun-loving, free-spirited guy who was very sensitive and emotional. I literally cried as I hugged my parents, although they were driving me up to school, along with my little sister.

We took the eight-hour drive, pulled up to the campus, saw the football field, the facilities, and everybody getting out of their cars, going in for the first time. I looked at my mother and my father, and they looked back at me. My sister was crying, because her big brother was not coming back home with her; I stepped out of the car, gazed back and said, "See y'all later." I had found my new home I was so excited. This is why I had put all that effort and time into high school. Moreover, training had brought me to this place, and I was excited to be there. In spite of leaving New York upset and crying, eight hours later I was in Maine. I felt at home."

From the first time I walked onto the campus and met the guys, this was my home. I'll never forget, after the first couple of days in camp, I said to myself, "These are some of the biggest people I've ever seen in my life." I mean, these guys were humongous, and it was, "Welcome to division one ball." one night I was on the phone at around 10 pm talking to my girl, all excited about my new adventures, and how the camp was going. I must have been talking kind of loud, because a rather big lineman came out of his room and said, "I'm going to break this phone over your head if you don't get off the goddamn phone, frosh" (which meant freshman). I kindly whispered to my girl that it was time for me to cut this conversation short, because there was this guy who was built like a Maytag refrigerator about to break the phone over my head. Surprisingly, besides that one incident, I got along with everybody. I was dropped off into a state I had never heard of before, into a situation where there weren't many African Americans, but I was feeling pretty good. It never bothered me. There were some racial incidents, though, which I was expecting. For example, run in with cops at gun point, a stand down with a fraternity, a brawl at a night club, as well as people staring, and then grabbing their pocketbook, or locking their doors when you walked by their car. Ironically, that stuff never bothered me, because I felt being from Brooklyn, the ultimate inner city, you were supposed to do that lol. It's so funny, just to show you the type of person I was; four days into camp, I met a brother on campus, (a black guy). Like

I said, it wasn't that many of us out there at the time. I think it had to be 98% white; or it sure felt like that, and there may have been 15 to 20 African American students in total--mostly athletes. In addition, there were a few students from Bangor, Maine, and a few Africans.

Anyway, I met a brother on campus, and I was like, "Yo, so where do you hang out? What's there to do around here?" he said, "They got this one club that everybody goes to called the Bounty." now, I'm four days into camp, and just to show you the free spirited, self-assured knuckle head I was, I said, "Yo, pick me up tonight. I'm going to climb out the back window." I wanted to check out this club. He looked at me and said, "You sure you wanna do that?" I said "Absolutely." So, he came and got me that night.

My roommate thought I was crazy; and I was actually insane for even thinking about doing something like that four days into camp my freshman year.. But I was this free-spirited person that wanted to know where the fun was. It was definitely stupid, but I did it. I snuck out the back window, went to the club, and got in because, of course, coming from New York and being from Brooklyn the ultimate inner city, I already had a fake ID. That goes without saying. You've got to have a fake ID in New York. And so, I got in, this was the one club they had, and they were playing top 40 music, and I was like, "All right, all right.". It's not hip hop but somethings is definitely better than nothing.

Suddenly, out the corner of my eye, I noticed a familiar looking man, I said, "Is that one of the coaches? oh, shoot." so now, I have to sneak out. I had been there for about an hour. I think the coach may have seen me, but he never said anything while we were there. We snuck out the club, and I got my butt back to campus, jumping in through the back window, just like I left, and nobody ever said anything. As a freshman, I decided to sneak out and go to the clubs more than once... but that was just the kind of person I was.

Camp went well. I really liked my teammates and made friends. I gravitated to, and got along with the upperclassmen, and even the big star at the time. He's still probably the number one running back that would come out of the University of Maine. He got drafted to the pros. While he was there, he gave me the nickname "Lunch meat." My teammates still call me that even today when we communicate on social media. I used to hang out with him, and a lot of the other upperclassmen when I was a freshman.

The season went well, or so I thought. The issue was with the coaches and my personality. They could not deal with my type of character, I understand it now, after talking with one of the coaches many years later... Many of these coaches were young at the time, and they were use to dealing with New Englander kids, which was a far cry from how and where I was from. Recently, I spoke to the guy who recruited me and told him I was writing a book. He explained to me that the head coach purposely had him specifically recruit the urban kids from Jersey and Long Island. They saw the potential value in those athletes, but I think the coaches were not mentally prepared to deal with what came with an urban inner-city athlete.

I took two trains and a bus to Queens every day from Brooklyn to go to a Catholic high school. My parents moved to Long Island before my senior year to facilitate my commute to Holy Cross High School. However, I grew up seventeen years in Brooklyn. Brooklyn is the ultimate inner city, and we've got that Brooklyn swag. Then, to top it off, having that Brooklyn swag, as well as being an artist trapped in an athlete's body, I was just a completely outgoing, free-spirited, super confident, self-assured guy. In retrospect, the coaches had a problem with me because they were just not used to dealing with athletes, with my kind of personality.

I'll never forget; I didn't play my freshman year, but I was on the scout team, and I took that very seriously. What happens on the scout team, is they run the offense of the other team to get our team ready for Saturday's game. So, I would run the other team's offense, and at the time, we had the number one defense in the Yankee conference. I literally use to run up and down the field on them. I was breaking tackles and making cuts; I mean, the defensive team's coaches would be pissed, yelling from the side lines, "Get him, goddammit." the coaches were so aggravated; but ultimately, the upperclassmen appreciated how hard I was working, because it was getting them better and preparing them for Saturday. I had nothing but love from the upperclassmen.

I remember at the end of the year, at the end of the season, we have our evaluation. Now, I go in thinking, "Yo, the coach is going to say, 'we love you, and we can't wait to get you on that field. You're going to be one hell of a ballplayer. Thank you very much for doing what you did on the scout team.' Again, I didn't play one down, but I was a significant part of that team, and we were Co-Yankee conference champions in my freshman year.

I wear a championship ring to this day because, to me, it represents sacrifice and belief in something bigger than myself, which is a team. Although I didn't play one down, I was an integral part of that team, because I got them ready and worked my ass off. I learned everybody has a role on the team to play. In order to be successful, everyone has to play their role to the best of their ability, even if it's not the role they want. I love to bang, and I loved the physical contact of the game, so I had a blast going up against the number one defense in the Yankee conference. Anyway, I get into the meeting, sit down with confidence, and the coach stands up and says, "If you don't stop acting like a clown, we're going to send you on the first plane smoking out of here." to say the least, I was completely flabbergasted. At that point, I had no idea that they had a problem with my personality. I had gotten along with everybody, but here I have this coach telling me everything I didn't think he was going to tell me. I thought, and was ready to hear, "You did a great job." they seemed too eager to shut me down.

From that point, I decided that I wouldn't change my personality because I believed that I was a gift from God. I went, and I worked even harder. I continued to labor even harder in the gym, even strengthening techniques with my plays, and pressed deeper to hone in with skills work. I'd focus a great deal on catching the football, to be that triple threat out of the backfield. I did whatever I could do to be the best I could possibly be. When we came out of spring practice, spring ball, going into my sophomore year, I scored a touchdown during the blue-white game, and I came out of spring ball in the starting position. Then, I went home and trained my butt off even more. However, I never changed my personality, all right.

I came back the next year, after that summer camp, in the starting position. The camp was going well, or so I thought. It was a really tough camp; coaches were working our asses off. We had a televised game, the first game of the season, and the coaches seemed to be determined to run us into the ground. I guess it was a lot of pressure on them, after coming off a championship year to produce; and you could see it in how they were working with us. It was surely tough, but I still maintained that free-spirited, fun-loving self-assured guy who was comfortable in his own skin. The coaches, I think, always thought I was playing this role trying to be the funny guy and trying to be this free-spirited guy when all I was doing was just being myself.

I mean, in retrospect, I used to do things like I'd walk around in a fur coat that I had gotten from this flea market in Maine. I called it the Joe Namath fur coat. I hung out a lot of times with nothing but girls. I wore red leather pants and a cumber bun. I would come to a meeting in a bright yellow bath robe my parents gave me. I just was out there with my fashion, and at the time, football players weren't really seen like that. Most football players walked around in sweats and jeans. I walked around in leather pants, a fur coat, and yellow robe. When I reflect about the coaches... I mean, I think I use to drive them crazy!

I'll never forget one time in particular when I saw the coach was pissed off. We had practice, let's say, at 10 o'clock. Okay? Now, I come in at 10; and, in my mind, I'm on time; but everybody else is already in the room, and they're just waiting. As a producer now, I tell the dancers in any of my productions when I produce a show, "I want you here on time, and that means early is on time. Being on time is late, and late is unacceptable." I can say that now. I didn't understand that back then. If the practice was at 10 o'clock, I would be there at 10 o'clock, or 2 minutes to 10. I used to come into meetings with that Brooklyn swag wearing my yellow robe, greeting everyone with, Yo, Yo, Yo. What's up? What's up?" then I'd slap everybody five, and people would yell out," What up, lunch meat?"

And that, I would imagine is why the coaches would 'go bananas.' We had a head coach who was a maniac; God rest his soul. He was a great guy, but super intense. He would constantly scream and yell, almost like a drill sergeant, intimidating all the players. I came from a legendary coach, Tom Pugh, who used a different approach. He motivated you psychologically and spiritually, which worked. So, I wasn't used to that loud, aggressive tactic, which I thought was funny as hell! I used to imitate him all the time during lunch, and my teammates use to crack up. Anytime he'd start yelling at me about something, I'd look right at him and smile. I wouldn't say anything, or ever be disrespectful; but I wasn't daunted by him. At one point, after a week of being yelled at, I got moved in the depth charts, down to the second string, and the guy they put in front of me was my man. We wound up being roommates. He wound up playing behind me during my junior year. The first game was on TV, and I was now second string. It felt like the coaches were focused on my personality, rather than nurture my talent, and the work ethic that I had put out there.

Sure enough, the first game I might have gotten on the field for a few plays, while we were on national TV. The team we played against, the starting quarterback, who had broken numerous passing records, was an All American. It just so happened to be my former high school teammate. Back then, we were on the same championship team together at Holy Cross High School. We were a tight family in high school. In fact, when I got into the plane crash in Rhode Island, his older brother heard about the plane crash on TV. He lived in Rhode Island and visited me when I was in the hospital. It was quite a game. We got blown out by them. I didn't sweat it. I kept working and working. Eventually, I started getting that playing time again. Looking back, that whole sophomore year felt like I was fighting an uphill battle that had nothing to do with my athletic talent.

There is another game I'll never forget. It was freezing. It was cold enough to be snowing, but it was sleet, rainy, muddy, and horrible out. And this was the second quarter. I was freezing. I was stiff. The coach observed one of the running backs who did something wrong and decided to pull him out. The next moment, the coach looked at me and said, "Theobald, get in there." in my mind, I said, "I know this coach just didn't say Theobald get in there." I was freezing too. I looked at the coach, the coach looked at me I was like, "No, I'm good, coach." he looked back, "Get your ass in there. God damn it." needless to say, I hopped up and got going. Lol!!!!

I had to take my stuff off and run onto the field. When I got in there, I said, "Yo, please don't give me the ball." I went in and did what I had to do and came back out.

Another incident that stands out in my mind was in Richmond, Virginia. We played against the University of Richmond, clearly a game we should have won, but we kept getting questionable penalties, and the head coach was pissed, to say the least! After we lost, the coach let us have it back in the locker room. He went off! I thought he was going to have a fatal stroke right there, because he turned beet red! A big vein popped out the top of his head, and in the back of my mind, I was thinking at any second his head was going to explode or burst into flames! He said, "You guys really sucked today; you stunk up the field! When I played, I sucked, but goddammit, I wanted to play!" He told everybody to go back to the hotel, get something to eat, and go to our rooms. He said, "I don't want to see anybody out of their rooms; you disgust me!" Before he finished talking, I raised my hand and said, "Excuse me, coach." He yelled out, "What is it, Theobald?" I said, "My grandparents and family are here; you think it's okay if I stay with them for the night?" He looked at the other coaches and team with this glazed confused look, then looked at me. In that moment, I'm pretty sure the top of his head popped off to make room for all the steam that was coming out. He went off, "Goddammit, you son of a bitch!" And then, he rattled off for another 5-minute tirade. That was the first time I was a little shaken; I wasn't sure what he was going to do or say next. I quietly went to my family and said, "Ahhhh… I don't think I'm going to be able to make it tonight. I guess I'll see you the next time I'm in Richmond."

Years later, I understood a little more about how difficult it must have been for some coaches. I get it more now, after dealing with different personalities from working with athletes and dancers. I believe (more so now) that work ethic and commitment trump a unique personality. People today are way more accepting of individuality than they were in the past. That's just how it was back then, unfortunately. I will never forget playing in the all-star games in high school. Coach Pat Kerwin, who coached for the Jets as a defensive assistant for years, and then advanced to Director of Player Administration for the NY Jets organization, came to me during a practice, looked me in my face, smiled and said, "Son, you're ahead of your time." That was after coaching me for just two weeks. I think one of the positive things that came out of this situation was that I blazed the path for other unique personalities that would come through the university in the future. I have to add that it was bone-chilling cold in Maine. My tears would freeze up, my nose, ears, and fingers would feel like they were about to fall off. When I would inhale, I'd start coughing, because the air was so frigid. It got so cold one day that I called home crying and said, "You got to get me the hell out of here; I can't take it, because it's too cold!" By my junior year, my body had adjusted, and I was good.

In my junior year, my body acclimated, and the coaches seemed to reconcile to me. I was now the starting running back and had a good year. And at the end of the season, the coach came to me; he said, "Listen, you're going to do big things next year as a senior." Just try to control yourself, son." At that point, in my mind, they were saying, "We can't beat him, so let's join him."

We had a losing season, my sophomore year, and a losing season, my junior year. That meant they weren't doing something right. Though I came away averaging around 4.8 yards a carry. The stage was set; senior year was my year to shine bright, my break-out year, or so I thought. I went home in January for break feeling sky high, happy to finally have my chance to be 'the man.' I trained my butt off and worked hard over winter break. We came back after the vacation to find out that the coach we had for three years, the same coach that said I'm going to do big things this year, had left to take a head coaching job somewhere else. Wow! So now, we've got a new coach coming in, and he, at the time, was the youngest head coach in division one history, another guy from the New England area. As soon as he came in, he and I clashed.

The first practice we had, unfortunately, I missed. I overslept. And, rightfully so, he made me run and did all kinds of stuff to me; and that's what was supposed to happen. The following week, on Monday, I got food poisoning and went to the hospital. By the time I came back from the hospital, before I could even explain to him what had happened, he had kicked me off the team, had the staff clear my locker out; and I was done.

Immediately, I'm in his office pleading for my life, begging him to reconsider, "Coach, you can't do this." and I'm crying. "Coach, I worked so hard," which I had, and this was my year, which it was. I was a senior. "You are coming here for one month. I've been here for three years, I've been in a plane crash, and worked my butt off, now is my time to shine, and you're kicking me off the team?" and I continued, "Coach, you can't do this to me." he then looked at me and said, "Boy, that's life."

That instant, I went from a boy to a man, because I stopped whining, and I stopped crying. I stood up, and in my head, I said, "Did this asshole just call me a boy?" I said to myself, "I'll be back," and I walked out of that room. At that point, I transitioned into a man. I really felt that free spirit attitude had left me because, from that moment on, I was a little more guarded. I was still that confident, carefree, self-assured person, but the free-spirited and fun-loving part of me that everybody loved, was gone. I'd come to a point in my life, when that part of me left forever, and I never got it back.

When I left his office, I had to make some serious decisions about what I was going to do. Was I going to transfer to another D-1 school? Where was I going to transfer? Was I going to allow him to take my scholarship from me, or was I going to fight? Thankfully, I had good friends in my corner. I had a guy by the name of Mark Gilbert, who was my roommate, I also had my best friend in college, Laurie McPherson. In addition, there was the Cook family. They were my refuge; and the family I used to stay with. Their daughter was another good friend of mine. This family became my family, and we're still family to this day. I used to go over there on weekends, just to get away from the campus and people, especially once I got kicked off the team. It became news when it happened. That old saying, "When you're popular, and you're up, you got a thousand friends, but when you're down and out, you're lucky to have even one." that's a very true statement.

I'll never forget going to the club, and not being able to get in free anymore, walking into town and people are whispering about you, and then you've got your teammates looking at you funny. People on campus are now talking about you, and now you're no longer this popular guy. Instead, you're this guy with the scarlet 'A' on your chest. I used to get away and go to the Cook's home to just chill with them. They also had three young sons: Zac, Jeb and Mac who I loved dearly, and I'd hang out with them, watch movies, and then come back to campus on Monday, go back to work, do schoolwork, and continue to train.

It was devastating for me, but I decided to fight, and I went back up there that summer and fought for my scholarship. I went back up by myself. I couldn't go to my father anymore. I couldn't go to my high school coach. This was something I had to deal with on my own; I had to handle it as a man. And that's what I did. When it was time, I sat in front of a board and explained to them, "Hey, how are you going to allow somebody to come in here for one month? I've been here for three years, working my butt off on a scholarship, I had food poisoning, went to the hospital, and I have a doctor's note," thank God, the ruling was in my favor—my scholarship had to be reinstated. That part was resolved.

But, since I got my scholarship back, the coach decided to tell me that I had to come back as a walk-on. Walk-on means you cannot come into the camp. You have to come in like you're some new cat off the streets. I had been playing for two years. I sat on the bench my freshman year, got playing time my sophomore year, and then as a junior, I became a starter. I was supposed to be the big star in my senior year, and you got this new guy coming in and doing this. He was trying to ruin my life, as far as I was concerned. I don't know if it was personal, or if he was showing the other teammates that, "You all better fall into line, because if I could do it to him, I could do it to you." I never felt it was a racial thing—like he was doing this to me because I was black. I felt he was doing this to me because he was a complete asshole with some power.

It was bad enough that I wasn't allowed to come to the camp. I also had to come in as a walk-on. So, what did I do? I continued to do what I do best. I worked my ass off. Although, that free-spirited part of me left; that confidence and the person that felt that God had my back, was still very present. I went home, and I worked out seven hours a day. I started pushing cars, jumping over hurdles, jumping over cars, jogging two to three miles three times a week and running hills . I ordered and worked out with rubber bands, and doing anything I could do to get that edge— I trained my butt off in the gym.

By the time August came, I was ready. I went back up there as a walk-on and immediately made an impact. Then purposely, I was transitioned from running back to fullback, where I'd have to block vs. running the ball. Again, he was doing everything in his power to ruin me. I never flinched, never said a word. Little did the coach know, I was also a devastating blocker, who learned to enjoy that responsibility in high school, because I love to bang. After every practice, I purposely ran thirty 40-yard dashes in front of everybody to let the coaches and the team know who they were dealing with. I particularly wanted to show the head coach, "You can do whatever you want to me. You will not break my spirit."

Every time I got in the game and did my thing, he would pull me out. So, again, he was blackballing, doing everything he could to keep me from shining. But, to show you how God is, and to show you how I knew God had my back, I got an opportunity when there was just two games left in the season. The starting running back, the whole season was a freshman. Now, hear what I'm saying. I started my junior year getting ready to have a big senior year, he kicked me off the team, and then he replaced me with a goddamn freshman.

The freshman was a nice dude. I used to take a lot of stuff out on him, and he didn't deserve that. He just came into a situation. At any rate, the freshman gets hurt. They've got to put me in now. Now, you've got to remember, I trained seven hours a day, and had so much anger and rage in me; I was ready. The first time I got the ball, I ran for 60-something yards and wound up running for 187 yards with three touchdowns. We beat a nationally ranked team. That was in 2 1/2 quarters, by the way.

The next week, we played Delaware, who had Richie Gannon on their team. Gannon wound up being a prolific quarterback in the NFL. We beat Delaware, who we hadn't beaten ever, ever! I ran for 183 yards and scored the winning touchdown with 14 seconds left. That's right. Instantly, the hero! I'll never forget the feeling of triumph, the understanding and realization that I am this gift from God, and God's got my back.

I'll never forget my partner, my best friend, my girl, Laurie McPherson, as well as my boy, Mark Gilbert, Chrissy, Sara, and Robin, they all had surprised me by coming all the way from Maine down to Delaware to support me and see the game. In the beginning of the game, I must have been in the huddle. Laurie and I had been arguing, or something. So, we weren't even speaking; but, when I looked up out of the huddle, I saw my people in the audience. Then I noticed Laurie had a big smile on her face and was waving… I'm getting goosebumps now, just thinking about it. I saw them, and it just gave me so much energy to know that I had my people with me, who had come all the way from Maine to have my back. That's what friendship is all about. Not to mention, of course, my family was also in attendance. I came out of that huddle, and it just gave me a little more energy to do my thing. I had an incredible game and became a hero.

I'll never forget the end of the game. Everybody was clapping and giving me dap and congratulations; at the time, my father had come up to me when he saw the coach coming out of the bus. My dad walks up to him, and says, "I've been wanting to tell you something." before he could continue, I put my arm around my dad's shoulder, I looked him in the face, and I looked at the coach, and said, "He isn't worth it, pops. Don't worry about it." and I walked off, and it was like one of those mean Joe Green lifesaver moments. We walked off, and in my mind, I was saying, "I was a better man than you then, and I'm a better man than you now."

That year, that experience, that triumph, became the thing that would put a stamp on the moment when I went from a boy to a man. It showed me that I could do anything I wanted. God had my back. He gave me the license to be comfortable about who I was because he showed me my worth, showed me that I was worthy. I was willing to educate myself, push myself, learn and study. I looked up information and got books on how to be a better athlete. That's why I started jumping over hurdles. Started pushing cars, etc.—to get faster, stronger, quicker and more explosive. I put in that extra work.

More importantly, I believed that I could achieve. It seemed that all the odds were against me. However, I persevered. He had blackballed me. He had taken me out of camp, made me come in as a walk-on, changed my position, and put a freshman in front of me. He gave the number I had for two years, number 33, to the freshman and I had to wear number 32. Every time I did well, he pulled me out, but I kept going; I put my head down and kept working, because I believed. I believed that I could achieve and was going to get that opportunity.

The time was running out during my senior year. There were two games left. It was halftime of the second to last game of my college career. Meaning, 2 quarters were already finished, and suddenly the referee signaled that the freshman was hurt and had to be carried off the field. They had to put me in. That coach was relying on me at that point. The same guy he blackballed, now had the keys to the first winning season in two years. All that work, all that sacrifice, all that time that I put in, those seven hours of practices, all that anger and rage I held in, paid off, because I ran for 60 yards, the first time I touched that ball. And now, he needed me.

As a result of that winning season, he turned around and left the University of Maine for another job. In retrospect, he came in, did what he did to me, benefited from it, and left. But it's okay. Due to this experience with him, I became a man. That situation is the reason I am the person I am today. There's nothing I can't do once I put my mind to it. I've got God on my side, and I have those five keys. I know who I am, I'm comfortable in my own skin, I know my worth, and I know I'm worthy of anything I set my mind toward. I continue to educate myself on anything I want to do. I surround myself with the people who have either done it before, and/or are currently doing it. I seek people that support my vision. I'm willing to put the time, work, and effort into whatever it takes to reach a goal.

Lastly, I believe I can achieve. When you have those five keys, there's nothing you can't do. There's not a reinvention you can't accomplish.

This is not a unique story, as I am positive that many other athletes have been, or at least felt they have been, treated unfairly by a coach. The belief they may have been just as good or better as the player in front of them, but because of whatever reason, they were not playing. What is different, is how I dealt with it.

I'm going to share something my dad said to me years ago that has stuck with me since little league. He said, "If you had a team and your brother, or cousin played on the same team, and you had to choose between your cousin, or someone just as good as him, and you wanted to win, who would you choose?" I said, "My cousin, all day. That's family." My pop said, "Exactly." He then said, "What about if someone else was clearly better than your cousin and you were trying to win, what would you do?" I had to think about it real hard, because I love my cousin. My dad then said, "You're trying to win a championship." I then said, "Oh, that's a no brainer, I'd pick the guy who was clearly better so I could win." Pop said, "Exactly." What that taught me, which has stuck with me since the little league days, was you have to be clearly better than your competition; so much better, that there is no other choice. Consider the possibility that if it's ever close, you'll ride the bench, because politics will never be on your side. He taught me, that it is what it is, and not to get upset with reality. You just have to do whatever it takes to be distinctly better than your competition. Those words stuck with me subconsciously throughout my athletic career, and throughout life. As a result, I became a slashing, hard nose running back who delivered the contact, a devastating block with soft hands, who could catch the ball out the back field, throw the football 65 yards, and the person who became the kicker and punter of my high school team senior year. I tell you this to say, "If you ever find yourself in a situation similar to what I went through, make up your mind to do whatever it takes to be irreplaceable, unforgettable, and clearly better than your competition. If the coaches have you training two hours a day, you train four. If they work four days a week, you work eight, and I know there are only seven days in a week; therefore, it's your job to find that eighth day. You find your competition's weakness, and you make them your strength. You make yourself clearly the better choice, and when you do that, God will do the rest.

This was the moment Lancelot E. Theobald Jr. went from a boy to a man!!!!!!!!!!!

They Haven't Made An AX That Can Chop Down A Dream

They Haven't Made An AX That Can Chop Down A Dream

They Haven't Made An AX That Can Chop Down A Dream

Lancelot E. Theobald, tailback for the University of Maine-Orono football team, has returned.

The basic facts surrounding his odyssey are now well known. A rising star for Maine in 1984, the 21-year-old senior got off on the wrong foot with new head coach Buddy Teevens last spring by missing two practices without permission. Teevens promptly dismissed him from the squad.

Teevens did leave a door open by saying Theobald would be allowed to walk on should he wish — 2½ weeks after the other players had reported to preseason camp. To nearly everyone's surprise, Theobald did walk on, and after working hard to catch up, has begun to see action again.

On the surface, this appears to be a football version of the prodigal son returning, a story with a neat, happy ending.

"He's a completely different person on the field," Teevens says now. "His attitude has taken a 180-degree turn from what it was. As far as I'm concerned, he did his time."

In reality, Theobald remains the independent, controversial player he has always been.

"I haven't changed at all," Theobald laughs, shaking his head. "My attitude now is exactly the same as it has always been. Coach Teevens thinks it's different because he never knew me then. The first impression is a lasting impression and he based everything on that first impression."

There is no malice in Theobald's voice. He speaks as an intelligent, articulate individual who has dispassionately analyzed his situation, plotted a course of action, and followed it. He does not blame Teevens, he merely recognizes the circumstances that led to the chain of events.

"I never should have missed

Theobald's view of his exile and return is dominated by the idea Teevens' actions stemmed from superficial impressions he gained from some of the Maine players who do not like the flashy-dressing maverick from Brooklyn.

"I'm a different person. I'm unique. I have a flamboyant style. On the field, I'm a total football player. Off the field, I'm a gentleman. I like to wear nice clothes and be with the ladies. I'm a confident person and some people mistake that for being cocky. And I refuse to change myself to suit other people," he said.

That independence is what has placed Theobald at odds with many of his more traditional teammates.

"I don't know if there's ever been a time I was considered a 'team' player," Theobald said. "Football has been my life since I was 8 years old. But I've always played it for me."

The decision to return to the team was a difficult one, according to the 5-foot-9, 200-pounder. He credits the guidance offered by Mark Gilbert, his roomate, and his father and high school coach for encouraging him to try again.

Making up the time he lost has been even more difficult.

"I feel I've got the offense down now," he said. "But it was hard work. It was like taking another course."

Surprisingly, he feels his teammates have accepted him. "You have to take into account there were some personality conflicts, but for the most part the team has been pretty supportive," Theobald said.

As for what Theobald has learned from the experience, he is icily pragmatic.

"I learned football is like a business. In the business world it's dog eat dog. Only

Chapter 3

Transition To Europe

I remember after our last game in college, it was all over, I had become the hero, I ran for 183 yards and scored the winning touchdown with 14 seconds left in the game, and we had beaten a team that we had never beaten before, that was nationally ranked with a guy by the name of Rich Gannon, who winds up being a prolific professional quarterback in the NFL. I remember the feeling of exuberance after that day. It was also the feeling of validation in terms of what I was experiencing. I had always said and was under the belief that if I worked hard, and put the time in, that something would happen for me. I believed that because I have faith; I know a higher power was orchestrating everything. My senior year in college, when the coach did everything in his power to blackball me, to the point where if I did anything that looked good in the game, he would take me out.

That scenario continued the entire year. It was horrible what this coach did. I mentioned before that in the second to last game of the season, the freshman running back got hurt, and they put me in, and it was just over after that. I ran up and down the field, but I always felt that God was the conductor of that orchestra. Once that last game of my college career was over, my journey was just beginning, because I had planned to go to the NFL—thinking that this was what God wanted me to do. I ultimately maintained the belief that I was supposed to go to the NFL to get that visibility, in order to truly do what he wanted me to accomplish. I felt that the NFL would give me the platform, and the visibility, to be a beacon of positive light, energy and change for the underserved in our communities across the country and the world...

Thinking back to when I played those last couple of games and all that turned around, it further supported my thoughts that a higher power had my back and was orchestrating everything. So, I said, "Next step is the NFL." First of all, I hadn't played, except in the last two games, and sporadically throughout the entire season. However, because I felt that God was in the driver's seat, I said, "I'm getting ready for the NFL." I literally worked out all day. I would train, take a few hours off, go back to the gym, train, run, rest, and then, run again. I was doing everything possible to prepare to get to the NFL. I had no idea how I was getting there. I actually received the Jerry Nason award, which was awarded to the comeback player of the year. The beauty of this honor is the fact that it was given out to one division one player in all of New England. It was voted on by the New England writer's association.

Each day, I was trying to figure out how I'm going to get to the NFL. I made some phone calls and sent films out. I got ahold of an agent in Boston, and he agreed to meet with me. Next, I took a road trip to his office in Boston. After our meeting, he agreed to represent me. He got me a tryout with the New England Patriots. The tryout was on the same day as my college graduation. I had to make the choice to either attend my graduation or go to this tryout. What do you think I chose? I went to the doggone tryout, that's right! I missed my college graduation and came away empty-handed because I didn't make it. I missed the only college graduation I'd ever have, robbing my parents of that moment; and, if I had to do it all over again, I would make the same decision. I felt I had to seek out the opportunity, because it was part of this journey I was supposed to be on.

I then proceeded to figure out what my next plan was. I decided to play a year of semi-pro football. I continued to work out and get faster, stronger, and quicker. The season started with a well-known semi-pro team that I use to watch play while growing up. The name of the team was the Brooklyn Mariners. Ironically, I had played with several members on the team from back when I had joined the Hurricanes in little league. It seemed to be a good fit, and I was doing work. We had two scrimmage games, and I was making plays. I had a few touchdowns and was looking sharp, poised for a great season. Before the regular season started, we had one more scrimmage. It was against the Brooklyn Kings, which was another well-known Brooklyn organization. I was amped up for this game because the Kings were loaded with talent. At the beginning of the game, I was ready to go in, then all of a sudden, they called the starting lineup, and someone else's name was called for the running back position. Needless to say, I rode the bench the entire game and watched him play; and as far as I was concerned, there was no comparison regarding his skill level compared to mine. At the end of the game, the GM of the Brooklyn Kings came over to me and said exactly what I was thinking. He said, "We scouted you these last two games, and there's no way this running back should be playing in front of you; come to Kings, and you'll start." In my mind, I had no time to waste by getting stuck in some political nightmare. I could hear my dad saying to me, "Son, politics will never be on your side." So, I made a decision that day. I was switching teams because, technically, the season hadn't begun yet; I had only played in scrimmages. I switched and was now a part of the Brooklyn Kings, a team I could honestly say had more talent in the skilled positions than any team I had ever played for. There was no comparison regarding the Kings' and Mariner's talent wise; however, having them all play together as one unit was a totally different story. We had a quarterback who was a Michael Vick prototype, before Michael Vick. Plus, he could throw with both hands. There were tight ends and receivers that had played in the USFL who had speed and athleticism. We were stacked in the running back and corner back position. Yet, we lost when we played the Mariners, a game I was looking forward to. The lesson I took from that was you can have all the talent in the world, but all the talent has to play as one unit. You learn to play as one unit when you practice together, regularly. We had practices once, or maybe twice a week, and we were lucky to have most of the guys show up. Come Sunday, though, the Kings were ready to ball. The Mariners couldn't touch the Kings with respect to talent and ability, but the thing they had over the Kings was simple; they played together as a team—as one cohesive unit. That running back, who I clearly was better than, had played on a team where they all had played together, worked together, and practiced together as one unit for years. That meant something and was worth more. As a result, they beat us. I stayed with the Kings for the rest of the season, and to my surprise, an international agent approached me after a game. He offered me a contract to play in Europe. What did that show? Again, it showed me that a higher power was orchestrating again, as far as I'm concerned. I had never even heard of an international agent; nor did I know they were playing football in Europe, especially in Italy. Yet again, I found myself on another new adventure, suddenly signing a contract to play football in Europe.

Believing that I was worthy of whatever it was that I was trying to do, being comfortable in my own skin, putting that time and work in, I was ready to embrace a new culture; I was ready to play some football. It was an incredible experience, not just the football, but also the experience of living and being a part of a new culture. I played in Naples, Italy. Additionally, I can't stress enough the love and affection I have for my teammates, as well as that organization, because first of all, they gave me an opportunity and treated me like family.

Among the things I learned was that once you go abroad, you realize it's a much bigger world out there, and you become worldlier, and more appreciative. Your eyes are open to a lot more things. You're grateful for what you have. I also began to realize that what you're going through personally is inconsequential, when compared to what is happening in the world. Believe it or not, one of the things I loved about Italy was seeing macho men who were affectionate towards one another. Males would hold arms and walk down the street together. You're talking about guys, six foot four and six foot five; it was natural as they greeted one another with a kiss on each cheek, which was foreign to me. I remember coming home from college, hugging my father, and saying I love you for the first time, because I saw my Italian roommate do that with his dad. We hadn't done that in my family. I knew my parents loved me, although you never heard them say it, you knew. I never hugged and kissed my dad until then, and he was so shocked his body just froze, lol. I hugged him and then said, "I love you, dad," and he mumbled something as a reply. I smiled because I knew he was completely thrown for a loop. In my family now, we hug and kiss and say 'love you' all the time—thanks to my Italy experience. I truly loved and admired that about the Italians. Even to this day, I still have friends that I keep in contact with and/or talk to on a semi-regular basis via social media.

I was convinced that the universe was orchestrating and wanted me to do this; I put the work in, and it's all about, once again, believing you're worthy of anything that you want, understanding and believing that you can achieve anything you want, surrounding yourself around people that have done what your trying to do, or support what your trying to do. Most importantly, putting that work in is paramount. By the time I got there, I had worked out, trained, and played a year of semi-pro football; I was in the best shape of my life. Now I was playing on a team; and despite the fact that we didn't win, not one game in Italy, we battled. I got beat up more in that one year there than I'd ever been beaten during any of the years I'd played football in America. I'm talking about from little league, all the way to college. I ran for over 1,000 yards in Italy that year, but physically paid for every single yard. I had to see a doctor to get painkillers, because I had separated the cartilage from my rib cage, after getting kneed in the side while getting tackled at the same time. Both my hands were swollen, as if I was shooting heroin. From purposely being stepped on, my back was taking a major beating, but I still wouldn't have changed this experience for the world. One of the things I decided to do while I was in Italy was to learn their language. I wasn't going to be there and force them to speak English to me. I wanted to be immersed in their culture completely. I went out and got a book. Plus, when I got there, I asked them to speak Italian to me. Little did I know that about 95 percent of the people I played with knew how to speak at least a little English. That motivated me even more to learn their language. Within a month of being there, I was speaking a little bit. By the second month, I was getting around functionally, and by the third month, I was speaking fairly fluently. Now don't get me wrong, it wasn't grammatically correct. The sentence structure was off, but after three months, I could converse without the help of someone having to translate for me.

My dad came to visit. And when he came, I picked him up from the airport. I walked around with him, communicating in Italian and driving. I saw him look at me with these eyes, and he was, I guess, quite impressed with his son, especially after all that I had gone through in Maine. I kept going, until I found myself in a different place; in Rome, at the airport of Rome, picking him up and transporting him back to Naples, where I was playing football.

Pop came, and as I said before, I wouldn't change this experience for the world, but I got beat up really bad out there. Pop saw a game where I had over a hundred yards but paid for every single yard. I was a running back who enjoyed the contact, and it would take three, or four guys to take me down. That became a problem; not for them, but for me and my health. After this one brutal game, the next day I was in the room, I couldn't move, the following day, I still couldn't move, and by the third day, my father knocked on the door and said, "listen, son, I love you, I understand you're hurting all over, but I didn't come here all the way to Italy to watch you sleep. So, get your butt up. We've got to do something." So, I mustered up enough energy to go out. We took the euro rail, to the famous city of Venice. I'll never forget, we brought a first-class ticket, or so we thought, and the first-class ticket gets you those rooms where you have beds where you can actually sleep.

When we get there, the conductor, or the ticket taker, comes in and asks for our ticket, we give him the ticket, and he says, "This is not a first-class ticket." in Italian, I said, "Yes, it is." in Italian. Now, I knew we paid for it or at least I honestly thought we paid for first-class. My mind went right to thinking he's trying to play us, and I started going *Brooklyn* on him. In a hood Brooklyn voice, I said, "Let me tell you something, sir. I know what I paid for, don't tell me I didn't pay for it," etc. I was trying to do that NY intimidation thing. He very calmly said, "Passport." I looked at my father, my father looked at me, and we both said, "How much did you say that ticket was?" lol. We weren't about to get arrested and go to jail in Italy to find out what the jail system was like. Needless to say, we paid the extra money and got in the sleeper. We arrived in Venice, and it was everything that I studied in art history. Now, I had taken art history as a buffer class in my freshman year in college and flunked it because I thought art history was drawing and clay making. Art history is just what it sounds like, the history of art, and it's difficult. I flunked it. The second time I had to take it, I got a c minus. But all the things that I had learned in art history I was now seeing up close, and it was absolutely breathtaking. In Venice, I remembered learning about its history and actually seeing a town that is immersed in water. The way you have to get around is in boats and this was actually real. We went to Florence and saw all the churches that Michelangelo had painted, which were real. We went to Rome, and the colosseum was still there standing thousands of years later; that's real too. On the Piazza di Spagna steps, we were hanging out and chilling. There was also the Fountain di Trevi. While there, we sat at the Fountain di Trevi having a glass of cappuccino.

I mean, this was all the stuff I had learned in art history that was coming to life. I actually experienced it for real. I felt so bad that I didn't pay more attention in the art history classes, because this was such an incredible experience. I just thought to myself, thank you for this incredible experience. I felt worldlier. I began to realize that the stuff that was going on in New York and in my neighborhood seemed so minute in comparison to what was going on in the world. The world is so much more of a bigger place. It just opened my mind up to worldly thinking. I came back a different person. Again, I wouldn't change this for the world. That experience is something you can't pay for. Well, you can pay for it, but it would be expensive, lol. These memories with my dad were absolutely priceless. Knowing how proud he was of his son, being able to hang out with him for the first time at a club on an American NATO base, is also something I will cherish and remember forever. Understanding what I had gone through, and watching me during that last college game, wanting to talk to that coach, being able to see me playing ball in Italy, was quite an accomplishment expressed in his eyes. It was just such a great feeling to know that he was really proud of his son.

Another priceless experience while playing ball in Italy was when I found myself face to face with the number one selling artist of all time, Michael Jackson. Way before I ever got into dancing and acting, my cousins and I would dream about being the Jackson Five. We'd often fantasize about having our own singing group made up of cousins and singing to adoring fans while we toured around the country. Of course, I was a major Michael Jackson fan and found myself suddenly a part of the Michael Jackson world tour in Rome. You see, the father of one of my teammates apparently owned a security company that just so happened to have the contract for MJ's bad tour in Rome, Italy, at the Studio Flaminio. My teammate asked if I wanted to work at the Bad Concert in Rome. Little did he know I had been working for a security unit at Shea Stadium and Madison Square Garden off and on, since I was seventeen years old! I gladly accepted the job and explained to him that I had done security for concerts at Madison

Square Garden. When we got to Rome stadium, they handed out our security shirts and assignments. To my pleasant surprise, I was part of the front-line security, whose sole responsibility was to be the barrier between thousands of adoring fans and Michael Jackson on stage. I was downstage left at the edge of the stage, making sure no one attempted to climb from the field on to the stage to hug Michael. It was the assignment of a lifetime, and I was amped and ready to do my job. It was a perfect night for a concert. People were screaming and yelling. It was electric; people were passing out and needed medical attention, and the concert hadn't started yet. Suddenly, there's this explosion, and everyone looks in the direction to where they heard the noise, and you see Michael 60 feet in the air, on top of the speaker, and the place goes crazy; it's about to be on! I started the night off with my back to the stage, facing the crowd, paying attention, and making sure there was no breach in the first line of defense. As I looked into the crowd, males and females were crying, jumping up and down, screaming at the top of their lungs. I'm watching this, amazed at what I was witnessing. Abruptly, downstage left, behind me, I can hear a voice faintly saying, "Who's bad?" Next, I can hear someone faintly singing. I turn around, and there's no one on stage. This now piques my curiosity, so I turned completely around to see what it was, and all of a sudden, what people thought was Michael Jackson 60 feet in the air was really a look-alike, because Michael was really downstage left about to be projected into mid-air. There's a second explosion, and immediately all the attention goes to where the explosion was, which was downstage left, right in the back of me. Suddenly, from underneath the stage, the real Michael Jackson was catapulted 10 feet into the air and would land on stage perfectly. He looked frozen—wouldn't move a muscle for what felt like five minutes, and the crowd, including myself, went wild. It was the most dramatic entrance I had ever seen, and he did nothing; he stood there with so much stage presence and dynamic energy. I felt like a little kid in a candy store and tried my best to be security but wound up with my back to the audience a great deal of the time, screaming like a little girl.

Thanks to those 5 keys, I found myself in Rome, Italy, 5 feet from what is clearly hands down the most electrifying entertainer of all times. I screamed and yelled so much that I was exhausted at the end of the night, lol. At the end of the concert, this amazing adventure was still not over. I was then asked to escort Quincy Jones and his family from his suite to his limo. I wasn't an artist yet but shook his hand and asked him if he enjoyed being in Rome. Many years later, I would see Quincy jones once again at a black-tie event for "100 black men" in New York City, where we spoke about that Michael Jackson bad concert in Rome, Italy.

I would make my way back to Rome again when I had a week off from football. I had a friend who was playing for a team outside of Rome, and I went over to hang out with him. This was my first time actually getting out of Naples, besides when my father came to visit. My man, Shawn Norris, was playing football for a team near Rome. His sister and a friend of theirs happened to be visiting at the same time I was there, and we all hung out together. Their friend wound up being a very famous actress who was on the " Martin Show " for years. Her name was Tichina Arnold, and she and

I became pretty cool acquaintances. She had her birthday party in New York. Lucio & Pietrone, who were my teammates in Italy, just so happened to be visiting and staying with me in NY at the same time as the party. My fiancé at the time, Lucio, Pietrone, and I headed to the city. After arriving in NYC for the first time, my friends from Italy found themselves embarking on this incredible American adventure. They were experiencing urban hip-hop culture and the young celebrity life in NYC, not from a tourist perspective; nor were they seeing it on TV, they were experiencing it in real-time, thanks to Tichina, and they loved it. Lucio would return to America again, the next time with his girlfriend, and future wife and of course, they would stay with my family. Following those 5 keys helped unlock a lifelong friendship that I cherish dearly. Lucio and my big bear of a teammate, Nuccio, would then visit many times afterwards. We always get together whenever they come to NYC, because that's what real friends do.

My football experience was great, and I wouldn't change it for the world. Plus, I truly feel the hospitality and love I received from the organization and teammates were priceless. I'll never forget this one owner, in particular, Senor Scarpati. I used to eat meals at his family's house, sometimes two or three times a week. His wife was just an incredible, loving person. I felt like one of the family. When I left, again, my sensitive side took over. I cried; I really appreciated the love, and the closeness I felt to them. Southern Italians are very loving and just beautiful people. I remember my man, Lucio, invited me over to his family's house for thanksgiving. As a New Yorker and what I would consider typical of a football player, I'd be ready to eat everything in front of me. I arrived at their home, and his family was absolutely wonderful. They started serving food, and I went to work. I started digging into the food. The first course came and I was taking second helpings.

And then, I started to really enjoy this thing called the caprese salad, which is tomatoes and mozzarella cheese, and I just filled up on that. Probably by the fourth course, I started getting full. Little did I know there were about another seven courses coming behind that—and it's very rude not to eat all the courses, that's just an Italian tradition. I didn't know that back then. When I saw the fish coming out, and then meats coming out, along with antipasto, and the pasta— oh my god! At that point, I was pretty stuffed, I was done. I was like, " Yo, I'm good." Lucio looked at me and pulled me to the side, and said, "No, you can't do that; it's disrespectful not to eat the food."

By the time dinner was over, I didn't want to eat, or even see food, for three or four days. I must've gained about seven pounds after that multi-course meal, because, like I said, they served me the pasta, the antipasto, the salad, the fish, the meats, the other kind of meats and the other, other kind of meats. After that, you got the desserts. I was just about ready to burst, I mean, I felt like a full-blown balloon; but, at the same time, I felt all the love and the passion that they put into presenting their thanksgiving meal.

In 2011, Nuccio was invited to do the coin toss at Met Life Stadium for the Jets game. Nuccio invited my wife and I, with Lucio to enjoy Met Life Stadium from the VIP club and field passes. That was another incredible experience I will never forget. Just walking out onto that field and then watching the game from the field was incredible. Not to mention the lobster tails, leg of lamb, steak, etc. In the VIP lounge. In fact, Nuccio and Lucio had just checked in with me the day before. I guess they heard that we had a storm in NY or something, and they were checking to make sure I was all right. That's the kind of relationship that came out of my belief that I had things to do and God was on my side. I found myself in Italy, and like I said before, I had no idea they even played football in Italy, much less ever dreaming about playing in Italy. It just goes to show you that the whole idea of believing, first and foremost, that you're worthy of anything you can dream of. Second, make sure you educate yourself. Thirdly, surround yourself with those people who have already done what you're trying to do. Or find those people who are willing and are going to help you along the way. You still have to work your butt off; and then, most importantly, you have to believe that you can achieve. I certainly believed that I had something else to do, once I finished my last game at the University of Maine.

My sincere faith that a Higher Power was orchestrating and wanted me to do something gave me motivation. I put the work in, which is a crucial part.

Once again, I can't stress enough about the importance of believing you're worthy of anything that you want, understanding and believing that you can achieve anything you want, surrounding yourself around people that have done it before and/or have supported you. Most importantly, putting that work in, that's the key, putting that work in. By the time I got to Italy, I had worked out so much and trained so hard that I was in the best shape of my life. I played on a team that didn't win, not one game, but we were competitive. I got beat up more in that one year out there than I'd ever been beaten in any of the years I ever played football in America.

I came back to America and got a tryout with the New York Jets for their upcoming minicamp. I had a 'less than impressive' forty-yard time and wasn't invited to the mini camp. I was devastated. I honestly thought this was the path I was supposed to take. At first, I decided to go back and play another year of semi-pro ball to continue working on my speed and agility. I played one game and noticed I was playing different; I wasn't the same player I once was. I wasn't playing with that reckless abandonment. I was shying away from contact. In one particular play, I went out for a pass and saw the defender coming towards me. Instead of keeping my eye on the ball, I turned my head to avoid contact, and another defender hit me from the side, directly in the front part of my helmet, which was legal back then. I was hit so hard that it bent the face mask open; it was enough for the defender's helmet to bust the top of my eye socket. It was so bad, I had to get stitches. Later, I started going over in my head how I got hurt. I came to the realization that I was gun-shy, playing scared, no longer that invincible player I thought I once was. It's like some boxers; once you get knocked out, you're never quite the same killer you once were. The beating I took in Italy affected me in ways I didn't even realize at the time. After half-time, I took off my helmet and shoulder pads, handed them to the coach, and said I was done. The coach said, "For today, I guess I'll see you next week." I said, "No, coach, I'm done for good. I'm hanging up my cleats." At that very moment, I felt it was time for me to move on. As I look back on it, I think that realistically, I'd given it my best shot. I'd worked as hard as I knew how and I took my talents to the maximum that I could take them. As I look back, God was doing me a favor. If my body got beat up like that in Italy, imagine what would have happened in the NFL, getting hit by the likes of Ray Lewis every week. I think God got me to this place in my life, and now he was saying, "Now move on. Take the tenacity, take the work ethic, take the belief, the comfort in your own skin, take those five keys and now implement them into something else. Figure out the next step in your journey." I left the field that day and never looked back. I didn't watch another football game or play or touch a football for about fifteen years.

They Haven't Made An AX That Can Chop Down A Dream

They Haven't Made An AX That Can Chop Down A Dream

They Haven't Made An AX That Can Chop Down A Dream

They Haven't Made An AX That Can Chop Down A Dream

They Haven't Made An AX That Can Chop Down A Dream

They Haven't Made An AX That Can Chop Down A Dream

They Haven't Made An AX That Can Chop Down A Dream

Chapter 4

Testing The Grounds Of Entrepreneurship

The next stop on my journey was entrepreneurship and having my own business. Well, after finishing football and deciding that I'd taken my talents to the limit, it was time to move on. My best friend, we were like blood brothers at the time, came to me and asked if I wanted to start a business together. We named it 'Lance Elliot, Ray Anthony Productions (LERA). We combined Lance Elliott which is my first and middle name; and Ray Anthony was his first and middle name. The business was selling sporting apparel and t-shirts. I applied those same 5 keys to this new part of my journey. Knowing your worth and knowing you're worthy of anything you can dream of. We thought we educated ourselves on how to do it properly.

We surrounded ourselves with people that were doing it or had done it before. We were willing to make sacrifices and put the work in. Most importantly, we believed that we could achieve. And so. The new journey began. The first idea was about how to make the t-shirts. We started off designing two shirts; and at the time, Batman was out. We came up with these incredible graphics called Blackman and Slick Tracy. What we did was hire an artist when we created these incredible designs. They were a spoof on Batman and Dick Tracy. We had a chain necklace that said, 'Fight the power' for Blackman and a five-finger ring that said 'Slick,' and a saying that read, 'We on the way believe that.' They were two incredible designs, and people were feeling both of them.

I still have those t-shirts today hanging up on my wall in a frame, they were the first official t-shirts we had. Next, how do we sell these hype t-shirts to the public? The answer was that we had no idea how to get it out there. So, what did we do? We hit the streets, we went to the village in downtown NYC, mid-town around 42nd street, and uptown to Harlem, selling these t-shirts out of a plastic bag. We'd yell out: "get your Blackman and Slick Tracy t-shirts!" We were selling out of our stock on hand and had to make more shirts. Soon, we started making shirt in other colors. We went to the Greek picnic at Jones Beach and sold out. Next, we started selling at flea markets.

Business was all right, but we were not selling in masses. We sold a hundred shirts here, a hundred shirts there. We were turning the money around to make more profits by making more t-shirts. Then, we came up with another spoof. My cousin, Marc came up with this one. Instead of "Don't worry, be happy, he came up with don't worry f### it." That became another t-shirt design that people loved. We were doing well, and it was exciting. We incorporated, making money, but the downside was that we weren't really making a profit, because we were putting money back into the business.

I had another cousin who was a designer. Well, he wasn't really a designer, but more of a tailor, and he made clothes. We got to talking, and before you knew it, he had put me in contact with a guy in Manhattan that he knew, a friend of his who designed and manufactured clothes. We then came up with the idea of making sporting apparel. We met my cousin's friend, who taught us about fabric grading, how to get the material, and also where to get the material. We started learning about sizes, patterns and how you'd have to go to one site to get the pattern and the grading. Then, you would have to come to him, and he would sew it; after you'd gone somewhere else to get the material. He taught us the difference between single stitch and double stitch. In addition, you'd have to go somewhere else to get the brand name tags.

The tags were used to identify who the manufacturer of the apparel was, and how to care for the product (the washing instructions). It was your logo. This is a Lance Elliot, Ray Anthony Production. This was our product. These were all things that we learned by being around people who did it before, which goes back to the rule of educating yourself and surrounding yourself with people that have done it before, and that's what we did. What we did was utilize the fact that I played college football to get in the door. We designed some t-shirts and took them up to a homecoming game at the University of Maine and sold out. I called Princeton University, where a former coach of mine was now the head coach, and I scheduled a meeting with him. We went to Princeton; the coach immediately introduced us to the head equipment manager, who had been with Princeton for a long time.

He gave us the contract to produce basketball apparel. The warm-up suits we custom-designed were at a time when the Princeton basketball was kicking butt during March madness which is a very popular basketball tournament, and they had made it to the sweet 16. They were wearing our warm-up suits, which was a big deal for us. We got contracts with Fordham University, Wagner College, Ramapo College, and Rutgers University. We were doing okay.

In the midst of getting these contracts, some of the other apparel companies started giving out free warm-up suits to all the colleges, or at least the colleges that we were also dealing with, not to say that they did it purposely to run us out of business, but I'm just saying. I will never forget what the coach from Fordham University said, "We really like you son, but unless you can do it for free, then we're just going to have to say thank you very much." That took a lot of wind out of our sails, but we kept going.

Thanks to our high school coach, who was the president of the Catholic high school football league at the time, we were able to do the playoff t-shirts for about four years for the CHSFL.

At the same time, I started getting disenchanted with the whole process. We weren't making 'real' money. I remember one thing that really kind of sent me over the edge. It involved a good Friend of the family, whom I'd known since we were little kids, and called each other cousins. I remember he was working at Red Lobster, the restaurant, doing crazy hours and saving money. He heard that I was doing sporting apparel. He contacted me, asking about how the fabric grading worked. I explained to him that grading is the process of creating a range of sizes, and that grading doesn't create shapes or patterns; it only increases or decreases the sizes of the original shape. He started sewing in his house. He and his partner had their fingers on the pulse of the hip-hop culture. I was in the area, I thought I knew which was more of the sporting apparel end. We wound up doing custom sporting apparel. That was the thing we thought would make us different, which it did. For example, I went to Princeton University, and we would design whatever they wanted, together. Then, we would go to our people and have them make exactly what the customer envisioned.

We were making custom sporting apparel, and they were killing it with hip hop wear. They were playing chess while we were playing checkers. Hats off to them. One thing led to another, and they had some great designers. The next thing we knew, about two years later, my father saw his brand in the front window of Macys on 34th street. At that point, our business had stagnated, and he had made it. I was like, *good for him*. I was truly happy to see him actualize his dream; he deserved it. They had broken through that glass ceiling; they had made it.

When you get to that level, somebody is definitely orchestrating and helping you to get your stuff out there. The one thing we've learned, because we also tried to get in department stores, was that they all seemed to have a thing called net 90, which is when you ship a vendor your stuff. Once sent, they have up to 90 days, three months, to sell your product(s) in their store, and then, get your money to you, for such a small business like ours, we couldn't deal with waiting 90 days. If we waited 30 days, we could be out of business. I began to get disillusioned and discouraged after a while, especially after we lost those college contracts.

Ray and I always talked about making sure we educated ourselves on what we were doing. So, we decided to return to school. We enrolled to take a course at FIT, which stands for Fashion Institute of Technology, located on 27th street and 8th avenue. I realized quickly that none of the information we were learning seemed to apply to us. Besides the net 90 information, I was in class, baffled... I was sitting with all these younger students learning about fashion but thought there was not anything we could truly apply to what we were going through in our business journey. In the end, we wound up not finishing the course. We needed help, but honestly, there was nothing to educate us or prepare us for this story I'm going to tell you next.

The next venture was at Ramapo College. We gave a presentation to the coach describing what we do as a company, and the coach gave us the contract. We then took the next step, designing a logo exactly as they wanted. After that was established, we then measured the team for sizes. We were very clear on our understanding of measurements, because we were taught exactly what we needed to do in order to get the proper measurements. We did it like clockwork—precisely how they showed us—inseam, outer seam, hips, neck, underneath the arms, shoulders, and across the back.

Ray was very methodical with all those measurements. We got all the information and handed it to the manufacturer. A major issue that we didn't see coming arose because when you have only 20 pieces, you get thrown to the back of the line. No manufacturer is worried about 20 pieces. They're usually dealing with 300 and 400 pieces at a time vs. small orders like our 20 pieces.

Many times, they said things would be ready at a specific hour, and then it became a back order to be delivered at a later date. Ray and I were sticklers about being on time. We were very professional as young black entrepreneurs. We felt it was very important to be early. We knew it was very important to do what you say. In one case, it was supposed to be ready on Wednesday, so we were planning on delivering the warm-up suits to the school on Friday. Come Wednesday, we arrive in the city to pick up the warmup suits, and they're not ready. We were given all kinds of excuses. Then they said, it's going to be ready; I promise you." It wound up being ready Friday, however, we were supposed to be on campus at five o'clock in Jersey; but, at 4 o'clock, he's just finishing, in New York. My doggone pressure... I didn't have problems with blood pressure, but I guarantee you that day I did! My blood pressure must have been through the roof. We were sticklers for being on time, which meant everything to us. When it was finally ready, and we grabbed the stuff and drove to Jersey. We probably got to the campus with maybe one, or two minutes to spare. But we got there on time!

The ball players were excited when we arrived. You could also tell the coach was very happy to see us, because he took a chance giving us the business as young black entrepreneurs. And we're happy because we got the merchandise there on time. The problem was, we never took a look at the goods because we were running late. We just grabbed the stuff and ran, not looking at the finished product. The team lined up, we gave everything out by name, and people walked off. All of a sudden, the first player yells, "Yo! What's up? This thing is too small! This looks like it's for another person!" then, you heard another person, "Yo! Yo, this can't fit me! My little sister can't wear this!" the next moment, everybody started saying that. Now, we hadn't looked at the product, and sure enough, the pants could fit me. These were basketball players. They're all about six-five and six-six, or taller. It was the most embarrassing situation. We said, "We apologize. We stand by our product. You're just going to have to give us a little more time, but we'll rectify the situation."

I was livid. We were both incensed. First, they were late, and then they gave us a product that was absolutely opposite to the measurements that we gave them. We methodically wrote down the measurements and gave them to the manufacturer, how did they come up with pants that could fit me, for basketball players? It just didn't make any kind of sense, so we went back to the manufacturer. The football player in me wanted to bash his head in. The Brooklyn part of me wanted to slam him up against the door and take his money, but I couldn't do that. All we could do was yell and scream at him; but in actuality, we needed him. He was our only source of creating this product. So, there was only so mad we could get.

We went back, visibly upset, and he apologized. Then he started mumbling something and everybody in the factory stopped working. They're all staring at us. The only thing we could do was say, "Listen, we got to get this product corrected—our name is on the line." At that point, we had to purchase the material again, which totally messed up any profits we could have ever made. We had to practically babysit this guy, constantly contacting him, to ensure he was doing the proper measurements.

Our only saving grace was the guy who was doing the work knew my cousin. I guess he didn't want to look too bad in front of his friend, because I think he could care less about what we really thought. It left a bad taste in my mouth. This was a hard lesson we learned. Factories deal in bulk. That's how they make money, producing in bulk. We were up here doing customized sporting apparel, and we were trying to undercut the market. We weren't making the money we should have, because it was too customized and in small quantities. And then, the profit we were making diminished, because schools were now starting to get free sweats. It was a good attempt, but I really started to be disenchanted by the whole situation.

I think with this particular re-invention, in regard to the five keys, we were missing one of the keys to be ultimately successful which was to educate yourself fully. I thoroughly believed that I could achieve. I knew my worth. We surrounded ourselves with people who had done it before. We were willing to do the hard work. We believed we could achieve. But, unless you truly educate yourself on what you are doing, disasters like the one we went through probably wouldn't have happened. We learned that in order to really make money using a factory, you have to produce in bulk. We'd learned that the idea of starting a customized apparel business might not have been the best idea, being that we had such small quantities, and not enough initial investment money; but we gave it a good shot. It was a good try. I was proud of us for having an idea, putting forth that effort, and following through with it. What we lacked was the educational aspect of the five keys. Fortunately, while selling t-shirts in the street, I met a guy by the name of Richard Willis, Jr. We just happened to meet on the streets while I was marketing the Blackman t-shirts. We became best friends, and actually, we are best friends to this day. I helped him launch a company called Mozell Entertainment Group, which brings me to my next reinvention.

They Haven't Made An AX That Can Chop Down A Dream

They Haven't Made An AX That Can Chop Down A Dream

Spandex shows the body that Lancelot Theobalt worked to build by pumping iron.

They Haven't Made An AX That Can Chop Down A Dream

They Haven't Made An AX That Can Chop Down A Dream

They Haven't Made An AX That Can Chop Down A Dream

Chapter 5

Introduction Into The Entertainment Business

Chapter Five, Next Reinvention, Executive Producer, Producer, Actor.

I helped launch Mozell Entertainment Group, a company that produces its own music, film, TV, docu-film, and theater based out of Los Angeles, California. As I said in the last chapter, I met a guy by the name of Richard Willis Jr., on 42nd street, in New York. I happened to be out there by myself on this particular day, and I was finding it particularly difficult to sell t-shirts. Cops kept moving me around. I found myself less than motivated, because my partner wasn't with me, and the t-shirts weren't moving fast. Then all of a sudden, I wind up meeting a stranger.

This guy came up to me and purchased two of my Black Man t-shirts. We got to talking, and he asked me who I was. I began talking about my business, and all the things that LERA Productions was doing. Then, I asked him who he was; and he went on to tell me that he had just sold a play that he had written. Then, he used the money to move to New York, and was going to NYU. He also told me he was producing another play he had written that was headed to California. I knew nothing about acting, or plays, or producing. The one thing I did know was that this higher power had my back and may have been sending me on this path.

I was at a point in my life where I wasn't really happy with what was going on with LERA Productions. It had nothing to do with my partner, who I loved and trusted with everything, and we had a great relationship; but I was watching my cousin do his thing with his company. His merchandise was now in Macy's. At the same time, we lost some of the colleges, because now they're getting their warm-up suits for free. I just got disenchanted with the business, unfortunately.

So, Richard said, "Well, if you're interested, I'm going to give you my number; give me a call." You're on 42nd street, and you're meeting somebody in New York City; you have to be careful. I went home, and it took me a couple of days to think about my encounter. I was just going over in my head, "Should I call this dude, or shouldn't I?" Well, what made me call him was that I believed this high power was sending me on this journey, leading the two of us on the same path. I trusted that he was giving me a sign toward my next reinvention.

I wound up giving Richard a call, and we must have stayed on the phone for two hours. I decided that I was going to jump aboard and go through this new, I guess, re-invention. At the time, I wasn't even thinking about reinventing myself. I was just going to take this road with an open mind. When we got started, the first thing he did was introduce me to the actors. He had written a trilogy, and this was one of the plays that he had written from the trilogy called 'Lamentations.' Now, he was taking writing courses at New York University and decided to enter the play in a competition in Los Angeles, CA. Immediately after meeting all the actors, it was like someone said, "On your mark…get set…go."

One of the first things on the agenda was trying to raise money to get a cast of five actors, plus Richard and myself, which made seven people, to LA, twice. We needed plane tickets, room and board, and then transportation to and from the competition. That was about $20,000. So, here's where I became an executive producer. Again, being comfortable in my own skin, knowing my worth, and knowing I'm worthy of anything that I set my mind to, I decided that I was going to help him raise this money.

One of the things we did was a little fundraiser where we'd have people that we knew, or met along the way, come to a meet and greet. During that event, we'd talk about what we're doing and try to get their support. When you do these things, you have to have a space. Then, you should have some sort of finger foods, beverages, like wine for your guests. This is a good gesture to show your appreciation for them taking time out of their schedules to attend. One of the first things Richard instructed was, "Okay, I need you to find people to donate wine and food, because if you pay for the food and you pay for the wine, then that eats into the money we just raised." He sent me out, saying, Figure it out." and I'm like, "Well, how do you get somebody to donate wine and food?" and he said to me, "A lot of times, all you have to do is ask the people who make it; they'll donate for good causes." I quickly learned that you have to get out there and manifest your destiny, by asking for what you want.

That concept was new to me. One of the first things I did was look around to see who makes this wine, a specific wine. It just so happened that one of the factories, at the time, was in Greenwich Village, right down the street from NYU, where I also went to school for continuing education. I knew that area well. I went down there and... Well, first we called them up, and told them we were producing an event to raise money for a production that would be competing in a national competition. Then we asked them if they could donate some wine. They surprisingly said yes, so I went down there; and sure enough, they donated about eight boxes of wine. And I went down to the village and picked them up.

I did the same thing with a very popular cake & dessert manufacturer. I called them, told them what we were doing, and then asked them to sponsor us by donating. By that time, I had become much more comfortable with asking for what I wanted. They also agreed to sponsor us; so, I went down to their factory in Brooklyn. I grew up in Brooklyn and used to live not too far from where one of their factories was located. Now, this particular company has a policy where, come to find out, anything that they make that's over a day old, or two days old, that they don't sell. They mark it as old. And they had no problem donating that; I mean, it's still good; but they just didn't sell it after a 24-hour period. They gave me a bunch of free pastries. I went from not knowing what to do, or how to get it done, to taking Richard's advice and just asking for what I wanted. We actually had the fundraiser with beverages, wine, and an array of different desserts. It was a great night; we raised some money, it wasn't nearly enough, but it was a great start.

Richard then contacted the airlines and surprisingly, got the airlines to help sponsor us by lowering the cost of each individual ticket, considerably. How did he do that? He just called up the airlines and asked. Then, what did I do? I decided to utilize some of my own contacts to help out. You see, sometimes you just got to get the ball rolling, then things just start to fall into place. Years earlier, I had met and actually had the pleasure of being around, and getting to personally know a very influential black man in America, Ronald Townsend Sr. I met Mr. Townsend Sr. through his son, Ron Jr. and another friend of mine that he used to mentor, Joby Smith.

Ronald Townsend Sr. Is the former president of Gannett Co.; he is a beautiful person; a genuinely nice guy. I got a chance to meet Mr. Townsend, and be around him and his family, which was so inspiring—just to know a black man who's achieved that kind of success in America. I gave it a great deal of thought; and ultimately decided to call him. I told him we were trying to get a cast of seven to LA for this major competition. Mr. Townsend hadn't seen or talked to me in years. His only question was, "Does this benefit me?" It goes to show you when you are sincere, present yourself correctly and surround yourself with like-minded positive people and friends, things like this can happen. I answered, "Yes, it does." I was hoping, at most, for a few hundred-dollar donations, but would have been happy with whatever he gave. Instead, Mr. Townsend said, "Let me make a call." When I called him back, he told me to contact this person, who would help me out. I contacted the person who happened to be the president of a well-known organization, and he agreed to meet with us. So, Richard and I drove to Washington, DC.

The thing about it is, when they see young men who are hungry, positive, and with a vision, people start to help you out. It was amazing to watch it unfold. This gentleman, thanks to one call from Mr. Townsend Sr., gave us a hefty check by the time we were leaving there. He wished us luck and gave us another contact of someone in San Francisco. He let us know, that once we got to California, the next contact would help us out as well. Now, we had money to work with, but still, it wasn't really enough to get seven people to California, twice.

In full disclosure, I was blessed enough to grow up surrounded by other positive black role models. Each of them showed me I could do anything I wanted in America, even as a black man, but they also let me know, it was not going to be easy. I understood there would be obstacles purposely put in my way to stop or hinder me. My dad was part owner in a very well-known club in NYC back in the day called "Club Pegasus." My Uncle Carl owned a well-known club in Brooklyn called "Mahogany" and they owned several apartment buildings. My Uncle Sam Belnavis was the first black owner of a Nascar. So, the concept that anything is possible was already ingrained in me, without me even realizing it. I believed the universe had aligned Richard and me on the same track, knowing we would figure out how to get to the finish line. We soon came up with another idea. It just goes to show you that if you want something bad enough, you can figure it out. And, if you believe that you can achieve it, you'll figure out a way to get it done. This was true the whole time I collaborated with Richard Willis Jr. We became very close, and are best friends today, because we were in the trenches together. We came up with what we coined "the $20 plan." What we did was write down the names of everybody we felt would be able to help us out, and then, we asked them for $20. In the midst of asking for $20, many people would give us more. Additionally, what they would do was start telling others about you and introduce you to other people that may want to help out as well.

Having a family that has accomplished a few things meant they probably knew other people who had accomplished things, because like-minded people tend to gravitate together. Richard went to his family, and they all contributed. I went to my mom and dad, and sister, who contributed. My sister got a few of her friends to donate money. My Uncle Carl, God rest his soul, had been a big supporter of mine ever since I was a little kid. We went to my uncle, who gave us $200. And then he said, "I want you to meet my good friend, Mr. Earl Washington." He was a big real estate broker in the Bronx. We went to his office; he wrote a $300 check; and then, turned us on to another one of his friends who wrote a $200 check. Ironically, Earl mentioned that his teenage daughter, who was no more than thirteen, or fourteen at the time, was an actor as well.

We started going to functions at nightclubs, and bars in the city. Remember when I said like-minded people tend to know each other? My dad and Uncle

Carl grew up with a guy who now owned another popular club in the city; his name was Billy Bowles. He became a big supporter. We just started meeting people. I learned how to be aggressive. "Hey, how are you doing? My name is Lancelot Theobald..." always following with a strong handshake, always looking everyone in the eyes, and then we would tell them our spiel. Occasionally, they might introduce us to somebody else. We even went up to the WBLS radio station, which Percy Sutton owned at the time, to see if we could get support. To our pleasant surprise, we actually bumped into Mr. Sutton, coming out of the elevator of his office building. We introduced ourselves, shook his hand, looked him in the eye, and told him what we were doing. He then made a phone call to Gary Bird, an on-air personality on WBLS's sister station, who interviewed us live on the radio. While at the WBLS station, we met another very popular on-air personality at the time, Jackie Bunch, who took a liking to us, and we became friendly. She mentioned us on air, a few times.

Now don't get it twisted; not everybody we ran into was looking to help us out. One well-known talk show host in particular, who will remain nameless, looked Richard and me in the face at an event and said, "Yeah, yeah, I'm not interested in all that." We said, "Thank you for your time," and he walked off. Although, he was known for being an activist and supporter of the people, he dismissed us quickly. That became a funny story and joke we would tell, and we called it, "we got poo pooed!!" Lol!! Before you know it, to make a long story short, we had raised the $20,000 and got a cast of seven people plane tickets, hotel reservations, and transportation to LA, twice. That's right, we got to LA and did the competition. We went up against Shelly Garrett, who wrote and produced "Beauty Shop," which was a really well-known play that did the theater circuit around the country. We went head-to-head with one of Shelly Garrett's earlier plays. It became a showdown between Richard Willis Jr. And Shelly Garrett. It was a well well-fought competition, with the California native shelly Garrett coming in first, and Richard Willis Jr. Coming in second.

While in California, again fundraising, to try to get food to feed the cast was part of our daily agenda. We met up with Roxie Roker; she was on the hit TV series; the Jefferson's. She played the part of the upstairs neighbor whose daughter, on the show, was married to George Jefferson's son. In real life, her son is Lenny Kravitz. We met her because she's a theater actress. We met her at the same theater where the competition was held. She took a liking to us and invited us over to her home. She also gave us money and food to feed our cast. Roxy Roker and Richard remained friendly for years, until I think she got breast cancer and died; but she was an incredible stage actress, and a really down-to-earth person. May she continue to rest in peace.

A lot of people really liked our energy and the fact that we had gotten this entire cast to LA, not once, but twice. We wound up coming in second place, but it was a crazy experience. I remember Richard and I were up for 48 hours straight, making sure our actors were taken care of. We were at a restaurant with a doctor who I had met on the street in NY, who happened to live in LA and work at Martin Luther King hospital. She was proud of us and looking to help out. She took us to a fancy restaurant. While in the middle of appetizers and conversation, we both fell over in our plates, face first, from complete exhaustion. She was like, "Guys, guys am I that boring?"

After that incredible life-altering experience, I realized that I really liked this acting thing. I had never been involved with acting, or this type of thing before; but became intrigued with, not just the producing part of it; but having the title 'executive producer' behind my name. This was because I'd raised over $20,000, to transport a cast of seven to LA and back, twice. Basically, that's the role of the executive producer, to finance the show.

Once I became an executive producer, I took a producer's course with Richard, to learn how to produce a Broadway show. That's when I was educated about where all the money goes—to unions. It's very difficult to make money in the theater industry, basically because a large portion of the money made at the box office goes towards paying the different unions. You have a limited number of seats in each venue, and there are just so many different unions. Fourteen different unions, to be exact, have to be paid. A lot of the money goes towards that. When it comes to the actors, unless you're a hit play like cats, or something like that, it's very difficult to make money as an executive producer. The first order of business is paying the unions, and then, your actors. But at least I went and educated myself on how to be a producer, specifically, how to be a Broadway producer, as well as how to be an executive producer. I had previously returned to school, after being selected for a special program at NYU called Sports &

Special Events Marketing, where I stayed on campus at Weinstein Hall and studied for a summer.

In the midst of educating myself, I was still very enchanted with acting. I really started gravitating toward being in front of the camera. Initially, I was behind the scenes, but realized my personality was pulling me towards acting.

Not that I didn't like producing and calling the shots, but deep down, I really wanted to be seen and acknowledged as an artist. I started to get that acting bug. Being a boss and being out in front as a producer, garnished respect, but I realized it wasn't enough for me, nor did it make me happy. I started attending class with Richard, who was taking a course at the Frank Silvera Workshop in Harlem, with a prolific writer by the name of Phillip Hayes Dean. He's passed away now, unfortunately; but he was a superb Broadway writer who penned Paul Robeson, which was a very famous Broadway play. These are the people that Richard was learning from; he was taking me to class with him, and I was around other artists at the Frank Silvera Workshop as well.

Phillip Hayes Dean took a liking to Richard. I think he noticed Richard's talent potential, as a writer. So, after class, we hung out with Phillip. On Monday nights after class, we'd go get drinks and chat. It was so funny, because the two of them would clash over different topics. They were two brilliant minds debating their point of view, and I would just sit back and listen. It was like being at a tennis match. Richard was young but had an older spirit. It seemed like he had been here before; it felt like he was chatting with a colleague, and not his professor, or mentor. In class, Richard always listened and learned, but outside of class, they would go at it. To me, it was amazing to watch. It taught me to respect and honor my teachers. I knew I must get that knowledge and education, but that doesn't mean I have to agree with their ideology, or politics. These are the kind of people that I was around, watching, and learning from. One thing led to another; he was studying at the Frank Silvera Workshop and decided to have a reading of one of his plays. We had an opportunity to do something for one of our generous supporters. I mentioned before that Earl Washington's daughter was an actress. Richard had her read for one of the roles opposite Kahlil Kane, who wound up being one of the lead actors in the iconic hip-hop movie, "Juice" with Tupac. Earl Washington's daughter is Keri Washington from the hit TV series "Scandal." It's truly interesting how people and things turn out. By this time, I was convinced I wanted to be an actor. My very first acting coach was Pat White from the Frank Silvera workshop. She taught me privately. Richard then brought in a friend of his to teach a group of us privately as we started doing stage readings of different plays that Richard wrote or produced.

To reiterate, one of the keys is to educate yourself fully. I have to acknowledge, being a part of Mozell Entertainment Group has been an educational process. This journey included: how to raise money, how to produce, how get things done, acting technique, artist development, storyboarding, and development of original show content. I was one of the producers along with Richard Willis Jr., Vinny Brown, former program director at 98.7 Kiss FM, Dedra Tate, former president of Motown Records, and Mike Baril, former promotional director of Sony Music on the Propmasters show. This was a TV show we created and produced for the legendary DJ Red Alert. Unfortunately, it didn't go to air, but these were the people I was meeting each week and collaborating with; it was an incredible journey and a tremendous learning experience.

Mozell Entertainment Group produced the hip hop artist, Reyn's entire catalog of music, which includes songs produced by the legendary EZ Mobee. Not only his music, but Mozell also produced his tour, where I was one of the choreographers. They were producing his music videos where my choreography and I were featured. Mozell has also done docu-films, and docu-dramas where I was featured. Plus, there were Janet Jackson & Hank Aaron tributes where I did voiceovers and commercials. Richard wrote and produced a film called, "At the Top of the Pyramid," where I was the choreographer and had a small role. "Middle-Class Black Folk in Da Claire De Lune" was a theatrical tour where I danced/choreographed and was one of the main characters. Being a part of Mozell Entertainment Group, has laid an incredible foundation for me, and has educated me on the entertainment business from behind the scenes, to in front of the camera. Mozell Entertaiment Group is responsible for kick-starting the second act in my journey called life, and I am forever grateful.

Right before I met Richard, I applied and was chosen for a marketing and special events program at NYU. I actually went back to school for a summer and stayed on campus at Weinstein Hall at NYU.

Ironically, Richard was attending NYU at the same time. I was so happy to be chosen as a recipient of this program. I wanted to educate myself on the ins and outs of special events marketing. All the things I did with LERA Productions and Mozell Entertainment Group would help to prepare me to be an executive producer/producer for my own productions. I went on to produce a show called "Hip Hop Fusion." It was a sold-out show I did for four years, utilizing all that education and knowledge I had obtained through all the things I did prior. I combined all the different elements and styles of hip hop dance; break dancing, popping, locking, krumping, tutting, and foot work, fused them together with the different dance styles: ballet, modern, jazz, tap, flamingo, salsa, Irish clogging, along with rappers, singer, and added comedians.

I'm also super proud to say as of July 11th, 2021, a film that I co-produced, choreographed, and starred in, along with Eric Roberts and Lindsay Johnson, is out on many streaming platforms worldwide: Amazon Prime, Apple Music, iTunes, Google, Fandango, and Microsoft.

I employed all the knowledge, information, and education from Open End Repertory Theater & Fred Sciaretta, Ted Bardy's acting school, Second City Improve, and years of being a part of Mozell Entertainment Group. I channeled that education into this product. I'm very gratified to announce that the name of the movie is, "Eddie" (2020), and it's been released worldwide; please go out and support it.

Anything you can conceive, you can achieve when reinventing oneself, by following these five keys:

1. Be comfortable in your own skin, know your worth, and know you're worthy of anything your mind can conceive, you can achieve.

2. You must, like I continue to say, educate yourself fully, get as much information on whatever you're trying to do, and you can never educate yourself enough.

3. Surround yourself with those people who have accomplished what your trying to do, volunteer your services if you have to, so that you can learn and be around those that have been successful at your goals and dreams.

4. You got to put that work in. You've got to be willing to sacrifice and do whatever it takes to be the best you could possibly be.

5. This is the most important; you've got to believe that you can achieve and understand; there's one formula for success, dedication, desire, and discipline is the only formula for success.

I acquired all that information, all the studying, including the class on Broadway, and the fortune of being around Richard, producing these plays. When it came time for me to produce my own shows, it was a no-brainer. I've produced five different productions—sold-out productions. I've choreographed 10, or 11 scenes for the film At the Top of the Pyramid. I created and directed 'Momz-N-Da Hood', America's and the world's first professionally choreographed group of hip hop/break dancing mothers floating in their 50s & 60s. Www.momzndahood.com

This all was possible because I followed those keys. Among them, is the fact that I surrounded myself with the people that did it best. Richard is brilliant at producing, and he's gifted at writing. I just sat back, watched him, and soaked up information to incorporate later. Anything I do, anytime I'm working with anyone, I always refer back to all the lessons that I've learned and experienced.

They Haven't Made An AX That Can Chop Down A Dream

They Haven't Made An AX That Can Chop Down A Dream

They Haven't Made An AX That Can Chop Down A Dream

They Haven't Made An AX That Can Chop Down A Dream

Chapter 6

The Four-Year Dance Intensive

Chapter Six, The Four-Year Intensive From Exotic Dance To Professional Dance.

A friend of mine from high school and his partner were promoters. They were preparing for a party with exotic dancers, and we bumped into each other at a club. He said, "Yo, you would do well. The ladies would like you. You ever thought about dancing?" My response, "No." I had never imagined myself as an exotic dancer, but it did spark my interest. I, of course, am comfortable in my own skin, I believed I could do anything I put my mind to, and I believed the universe had my back, orchestrating everything. So, I decided to do it!! It was at a club called Spectrums on Long Island. It would be my first time ever being on stage. I was excited, because I knew I wanted to be on stage, based on my experiences with Mozell Entertainment Group. I put together a costume, then went down to the club, and I was hooked. It was the same kind of electricity that I used to feel when I was playing football, that excitement of girls going crazy, that frenzy of the crowd, and then you have these buffed men dancing, the club is popping, the music is loud, and it was just electric—I was just hooked.

I'll never forget, when I first went out a little nervous, but being comfortable in my own skin, I mentally channeled my confidence to the surface. I watched these guys perform; they were acrobatic and could dance. I mean, an extremely, extremely talented bunch of guys:

So, I went out there, and since I was always a club dancer, I could really move to house music, I did my thing. I remember the first time I got out there, and girls started screaming; I started house dancing, then jumped over this banister and landed on a table and broke it in half. The girls went crazy, screaming, laughing I was hooked, and just fell in love with that energy.

After that show, I was determined to figure out where the next show was. I started working on my costumes, and my routine. One of the promoters had a club called Tribeca, and they started having shows there once a week. I went down and met with him, and he remembered me from the previous show I did. My second show was at Tribeca. I did well. Once I did well, it became a weekly thing. I was a creative person, so those first few years, I had crazy props—a bed, chair, towel, squirter, roses, etc. I needed someone to help me. So at first, I asked my man, Howie Hudson, to manage me and roll with me, and he did a couple of shows. And then my little cousin Marc Theobald had come home from college, he'd just graduated, and was looking for something to do. I said, "Marc, how would you like to just manage me as I'm dancing?" by this time, I had been getting more gigs, and it was exciting. Marc came down to one show, and he was like, "Hell yeah." his job was to roll with me to the different shows, and on cue, he'd come out, bringing my props, because I had a large assortment back then. At the time, exotic dancing was on the uptick, and it was crazy! I mean, we'd get 300 girls in the club on a weekly basis.

I understood that being comfortable in your own skin, knowing your worth, and knowing you're worthy, sets you up to be and feel a certain way. I watched the people around me and observed what they did, then dedicated my time to practice and working out, to get my body and routines ready. The most important thing was I believed I belonged there. Soon, I started rising in the ranks among the dancers, in terms of being one of the top dancers, after a few years. I will never forget the competitions. In the first big competition, I must've come in third place. And by, let's say, two years in, I had beaten the top dog out there at the time. And then, I became the number one dancer on Long Island. I started meeting other promoters. Before you knew it, I was doing all kinds of gigs.

So, my cousin is rolling with me, and I guess you can say managing me. One time, we were at a big competition on Long Island, and his job was to come out on cue, bring the bed, the blanket and some other props. It was jam-packed, and it was a competition. At the moment the cue music came in, I was waiting for the bed. When I looked, there was no bed, no Marc. What the heck is going on? I looked again, and Marc was busy talking to some girl; she was pinching him and pulling on him. I was like, "Yo Marc, what the..." he responded with, "I'm sorry, I'm sorry."

He'd brought the bed out late. He wasn't used to all the girls. It was just so many girls. They were screaming and yelling. When they get crazy and amped up like that, they started pulling on him and grabbing his butt. Instead of paying attention to me and the cue, he started paying attention to the girls talking to him. That happened a few times…the ironic thing is that he would later become a comedian… he graduated from a prestigious HBCU with a marketing degree, and eventually chose to tell jokes for a living. My aunt was not too happy with me at first, but she's okay now I guarantee you. They had comedy night on Fridays at Tribeca. I knew the promoter and got him his first gig. I'm proud to say my little cousin is now a successful stand-up comedian, writer, and co-executive producer of the hit TBS series starring Tracy Morgan, "The Last OG."

I was climbing up the ranks of exotic male dancers. I was one of the top dancers coming out of Long Island; I started getting gigs in Brooklyn, Queens, and the Bronx. I started doing the Spanish circuit and the gay circuit; then, I hooked up with a group called the A-Team international, with all these beautiful body cats and a model.

I remember we performed at Sinbad's jazz fest, in St. Thomas. They mobbed us in town. The promoter had us stand on the back of a pickup truck and ride through town, handing out flyers. Suddenly, people started running out of the stores. Girls jumped out of their cars and started grabbing us and taking pictures. It got so bad the cops had to come to clear the street because the people had shut down the traffic, trying to get to where we were.

It was like we were Michael Jackson and the Jackson 5, or something. It seemed like a whole island of ladies had converged down on us, and we loved it. The promoter also had a nice size boat. He had all of us stand spaced out across the front of the boat. Then, he proceeded to steer the boat across the water, parallel to where Sinbad was having a beach party. People noticed the boat with us standing on it, and literally, it looked like the whole beach was packed with thousands of people who started running towards us and following the boat. It looked like a sea of ants running towards food. We anchored in the water and walked onto the beach and once again, got mobbed with people taking pictures and pulling and hugging us. So much so, that Entertainment Tonight, who was there covering Sinbad's jazz fest, approached us to get an interview live on their show, asking who we were. Two days later, we took a boat to St. John's, then flew to St. Croix, where we had a few shows.

St Croix was the first place where we were met with hostility from the men on the island, individually and in groups. So much so, that we had to scale back on promoting in the malls on the island. At least a half dozen times, we were met up with hostility from different guys; then one group of guys wanted to challenge us. Ironically, we all were either from Brooklyn or the Bronx, and this wasn't our first time to the rodeo. We were talking junk right back and didn't back down. One of the dancers said something, and the guy responded with, "Wait here; I'll be right back." One of the other dancers said, "We'll be right here, bitch." They ran off. As soon as we could not see them anymore, we looked at each other and said, "Let's get out of here." We got back in that van and hustled back to the hotel. We may be from Brooklyn and the Bronx, but obviously, mama raised no fools!

We traveled internationally to Italy and Austria. I remember going to Austria, from Italy, by way of train. It was a four-hour train ride to Austria, which had a beautiful landscape, consisting of these breathtaking green mountains, as far as your eyes could see. We arrived in Austria, met the promoter, and had dinner. We figured we were going to hang out after the show and vibe with Austria's culture. Well, we figured wrong; because as soon as we finished the show, they put us back in the car, took us to the train, and shipped us back to Italy. We never got a chance to even communicate with the people.

I remember getting off the plane when we landed in Milan, Italy, and being stopped five times before we got out of the airport. I was the only one that kept getting stopped and asked for my passport. I was feeling targeted and singled out, so I respectfully asked the policeman with the ak47 machine gun in his hand if he spoke English. He said, "Non parlare english," so I said in a calm, nice tone with a smile on my face, "Penis in your mouth, and balls on your lips, bitch." The policeman smiled, looked at my passport, and let me go. That became the running joke for years, every time we saw each other back home. We found out later, while we were in Italy that I kept getting stopped because they were having a major problem with Moroccan drug dealers bringing drugs into the country, and apparently, I looked like a Moroccan drug dealer.

So now we're in Italy at McDonald's. Remember we are five good-looking American guys. All crazy jacked. As we get into McDonald's, and they're taking our orders, somebody asked, "Who are you?" and one of the dancers said, "We are American strippers from New York." why did he say that? Yo, the place went nuts! Somebody must have gone outside and told people we were 'rappers' from New York instead of strippers. People just started bum-rushing the store. Now, McDonald's is jam-packed. Kids started saying, "What rap group are you?" In broken English. We were like, "Rap group, huh?" Then, one of the dancers said he was Scorpio from Grand Master Flash and the Furious Five. The place went berserk! Some of the guys were upstairs signing autographs. The girls were screaming and grabbing at us. I mean, it was crazy, crazy. Again, they had to get the cops to clear the place out, because they had just completely jam-packed the place.

I've also performed in Canada. I was on the bus ride up to the border. Once again, I was the only dancer, out of six, who was detained for 20 minutes while they checked and double-checked my ID. By that time, I was used to being the one targeted and stopped at the airports, and border checkpoints. It was a crazy cool experience dancing in Canada. They had us doing radio drops at their popular radio stations promoting the show. Then they had us appear as guests on a live dance show which would be equivalent to our club MTV from back in the day. We had a blast; the shows went well. We had a meet and greet after each show, where we handed out pictures and signed autographs. Montreal loved us, and we loved Montreal. There were people of all different races standing in line for autographs. For some of the dancers, it was the first time they felt being a dark-skinned black man didn't matter. It affected their psyche so much that two dancers who I toured with, decided to relocate and move to Canada permanently. I saw one of the dancers a few years later at a show. The first thing I wanted to know was, what happened? How is it living in Canada? He said he was just here visiting, and he really loved it in Canada. He truly looked happy, and I was happy for him. Thanks to exotic dance, he found a place he could now call home, a place where he didn't have to feel the burden of being a black male in America. These are some of the unique experiences that I have had abroad as an exotic dancer...

Back in New York, my boy, myself, and one other dancer started a group called Chocolate Fantasies. In the beginning, we started promoting on Long Island, where I would do the promoting. We were killing it there. And then, we were the first to bring dancers up to Connecticut. On a few occasions, we used to travel up to Connecticut in a limo. One of the dancers had a friend who owned a limo company, and he used to love rolling with us. We would pull up to the shows in Connecticut in a limo which would totally add to the mysticism of these exotic dancers from New York. It was so amazing, because I would take a ballet class with kids, change clothes, get picked up at the studio in a limo, and head to Connecticut, where I would be taking my clothes back off, dancing for the ladies, and picking big girls up in chairs, driving the ladies crazy. I'm talking about all up and down Connecticut, starting in Stanford. We would go as far up as Hartford, doing shows on a weekly basis. Then, we started traveling to Philly and Jersey. Eventuality, I got with a friend of mine who hooked me up with a group that did shows down south. I moved to Jersey and was doing shows while living in Jersey with a girlfriend, for a few years. This was a time when I was at the top of my game as an exotic dancer. I was doing both circuits, the gay and the female circuit. Just in New York City alone, you couldn't walk down the street without somebody knowing who you were. I started making the rounds on the popular talk shows at the time. I was among the guests on the "Richard Bey" show, twice. On the "Phil Donahue" show, two African American exotic dancers and I were doing my choreography, and we went up against the Chippindale dancers. We beat them on national television. I was a guest on the "Roland Watts" show, and the late Joan Rivers television show on QVC. A producer from the Ricky Lake show approached me in the China Club and asked if I wanted to be a guest on the "Ricky Lake" show when it first came on TV. I asked what the topic was, and she responded with, "Men who think they are all that" my answer was, "No." It was a good time. It was a good feeling. Some of the people that I was dancing for, were major artists. You're talking about people on Broadway, music producers, actors, and opera singers. It was just an incredible amount of people that you might run into in NYC, after a while. This one particular person always used to say, "You've got something. You've got some talent." Always very respectful, he said to me one time, "Look, here's a phone number; I want you to call and speak to a guy I know. This could be a good move for you." I did it partly because I felt the universe was guiding me and that this was what I needed to do. So, I got in contact with the guy, and he told me that he was putting on a show that was going to be touring outside the country. He was looking for exotic dancers who could dance and pick up choreography. I said, "That would be me, and I'm definitely interested." What he was doing was taking exotic dancers, training them with the basic moments, and teaching them choreography. His name was Frank West. He was the artistic director of a company he created called the "Red Bone Dancers."

So, we started rehearsal in this incredible building in the middle of Manhattan with high ceilings. It looked like a place where Kings and Queens would come if they were here to visit. It was just that beautiful, I had never seen or been in an apartment building like that. Ironically, it was actually the apartment building of the person that introduced me to Frank. We use to actually rehearse in the hallway. After a couple of days, I started getting that feeling that I had when I took ballet class for the first time, years ago in college.

I took one ballet class and could not do the basic warm-up across the floor, yet in the club, I was killing it. A girl I knew who use to really enjoy dancing with me at the club convinced me to take a ballet class at the university. That's when I realized I really didn't know how to dance. I was a club dancer, but not a real dancer. Well, this is the exact feeling I was feeling with this choreography. It was taking me literally a month, a month and a half to learn what a dancer, or what I would learn in one day now. It was extremely frustrating; I know, for the choreographer and director, but it was frustrating for me as well. But we kept pushing, and we kept pushing, and I finally got it. We were ready for the tour, and the tour was great. We went to Puerto Rico, and we danced at different venues in Puerto Rico. It was well received. I really enjoyed myself; I enjoyed Puerto Rico, as well.

Then, we came back to rehearse for a couple of dates in New York City. In the process, I could see the frustration on the choreographer's face, because I just was not picking up the choreography quickly enough. Now, once I got it, I killed it, but it was a matter of being able to pick it up in a timely manner, so we could move on to other things. One day, he said, "You know, if you really want to learn to dance, I'll take you to a place where they'll teach you how to dance." I was like, "Really?" I said, "All right, well, I'm interested." a couple of weeks went by. I was like, "Yo, what happened to that dance school you were talking about?" he said, "All right. You're serious?" if you're absolutely serious, meet me in Queens."

I lived on Long Island. So, it was only about 15-20 minutes from me. I met him in Queens, and we went to a place by the name of Bernice Johnson Cultural Art Center. We walked in, and he introduced me to the artistic director of Bernice Johnson. At the time, it was Tony Marlborough. We met, and Tony told me to come back. I came back by myself and auditioned for him. Afterwards, he said, "I'm willing to give you a full scholarship; you'll train here. It's an intensive 4-year dance program. He said, "You just happen to come at the right time, because we were looking for some males, for this nontraditional student program." I wanted to know what a nontraditional student program would entail.

He said, "Well, you'll be taking anywhere from 14 to 20 classes a week. You'll be taking ballet, modern, jazz, African, and tap. You'll be learning different techniques in modern." I was like, "I'm all for it. All right, let's do it!" I knew the universe was sending me on this next journey. I knew my worth. I was comfortable in my own skin. I knew that I was going to put the work in. So, I was like, "Let's do it." he said, "The only thing is you're going to have to take the class with kids." I was like, "Kids?" he said, "Yeah, you'll take the classes with kids. We have a studio that's comprised of teenagers, as well as younger students." I hesitated for a moment, thought about it and said, "Okay, no problem, let's do it." we started a few weeks later, and the actual program started for us in the summer. Once again, I found myself doing something unexpected, but I knew a higher power had my back and was guiding me. So, two other dancers and I started the intensive program that summer. We began with a tap class, a modern class, and a jazz class. September came around, and the rest of the students started coming back. Now, Bernice Johnson, little did I know, was a well-known dance school. The studio was known for putting out some unbelievable dancers, choreographers, actors, and artists who all came out of this incredible dance studio in Queens, NY. We could start off with the R&B sensation, Ashanti, who was actually in my class. You've got Michael De Lorenzo from New York Undercover. He's an actor; he came through there. You've got, of course, the late great Prodigy Mobb Deep, who grew up there. Actually, his aunt is Bernice Johnson, his mother, Fatima Johnson, who was with the singing group "The Crystals." Valarie Pettiford, of Half & Half, who portrayed the mother in the television series, but she's an incredible dancer as well. You've got Lola Falana, Winston Dewitt Hemsley, and Ben Vereen, who I met and had a chance to talk to personally. He was active at Bernice Johnson. He came back to meet and encourage the students. Michael Peters was the famous choreographer for Michael

Jackson, but also was the choreographer for the hit Broadway Show "Dream Girls," as well as a host of other things. Lester Wilson, who choreographed "Saturday Night Fever," and taught John Travolta to dance. Frank Hatchet, who founded Broadway Dance Center, gave me my first gig as a dancer/tapper with the show he choreographed and directed called, "The Indigo Dancers" at the famous Kit Kat Club on Broadway. Kevin Jeff, a dancer from Jubilation, there's Chucky Epps, a well know Alvin Ailey dancer and choreographer, Obediah Wright and incredible dancer, choreographer, who attended Julliard one of the most prestigious artistic schools in the world, in addition to, Nasha Thomas former principal dancer with Alvin Ailey. There were a host of other people that have come out of Bernice Johnson. This was just to name a few.

I took that legacy very seriously, I wanted to be a part of it, and I wanted to be able to represent Bernice Johnson in the years to come. So, I went there to work hard, and was very focused. I was this muscle-bound exotic dancer who would break out in an incredible sweat, just stretching, trying to get my body limber enough to move like a trained dancer.

Saturdays, we'd have five, or six classes. I'd have to come to school literally with just a bag full of t-shirts; and then, a plastic bag to put each of the wet t-shirts in. Those are some of the things that I used to go through early on. My class was the last class before the studio closed down.

Bernice Johnson passed away in her nineties, and they had a great memorial service for her. People from different years came to pay tribute. I was so proud, because they brought our group up to the stage and recognized us as the last class, before the studio closed its doors. So, to be a part of that legacy, and to be a part of this incredible school, I've always felt that I was carrying a torch. I was going to take what I learned in school and utilize it all, so I could make Bernice Johnson and Tony Marlborough proud.

I'm telling you, Tony Marlborough put some of the best teachers in front of us. I had this one particular ballet teacher who really took a liking to me, because I was very focused. Theara Ward, from Dance Theater of Harlem. She was dancing at the Metropolitan Opera House and heard that they were having auditions for a show called 'Samson Et Delilah' with Placido Domingo. She got me an audition, and I actually landed a paid super position, and performed three seasons at the Metropolitan Opera House, performing in the production of Samson Et Delilah. It was an incredible experience, and I'm friends with some of the cast members to this day, thanks to my ballet teacher.

Dancing with kids taught me patience, first of all. And it taught me incredible humility. I'll never forget it. I'm in class, and I couldn't get a step. And, this little nine-year-old girl, after about two weeks, she said, "You can't get the step, stupid?" and I'm like, whoa, okay first of all, I wanted to wring her neck, but, of course, you can't do that with a nine-year- old kid, even though she called me stupid.

Never would a 300-pound teammate look at me and call me stupid to my face. There was too much respect. Yet, I had a little girl calling me stupid. It just really taught me humility, and it taught me patience. Then, every week, I had to deal with the front desk people. Some of the parents and teachers who did not like the fact that these three men who were new to the studio, were on full scholarships, and taking three times the number of classes than everyone else. I wasn't accustomed to the straight attitude and disdain. Every time I would say something simple like, "Good morning, how are you today? They may respond with 'fine,' but their body language and attitude said just the opposite. I would say, "Tony, what is wrong with these ladies?" I was so focused and determined to suck up everything that I was being taught. I made a conscious decision to kill everyone with kindness, by continuing to be pleasant and respectful. There was only one time I sort of snapped and gave someone a piece of my mind. Many years later, I figured out what must have been the problem. Many students had taken class there since they were three years old, and their parents had taken class there when they were kids. This was a legacy school, and suddenly, you have three new guys who were basically given 'the keys to the kingdom', so to speak. To top it off, two of us were grown men with no previous dance experience. It may have felt like a slap in the face to many folks, and to be honest, I may have felt that way as well, if I was in their position. Tony explained to me, years later, why he started this accelerated program for men. He said Bernice Johnson loved her male dancers, and he had taken over the studio at that time. There were no men in the studio dancing. He knew what she liked, and would have wanted, so he took it upon himself to go out and find men—and he didn't care what anyone else thought.

I remember every once in a while, Tony Marlborough would bring Bernice Johnson to the studio. She was this incredibly beautiful, elegant lady that was one of the few darker-skinned dancers at that time who was allowed in the "Cotton Club." She was married to Bud Johnson, who was a legendary jazz saxophonist. She had this incredible legacy and owned her own dance school for over forty years. She'd walk into the studio, and the entire studio would just stop.

Everybody would stop what they were doing when she'd come in. The teachers down to the students, would just be in awe of this lady. Unfortunately, I wasn't there at the time when she was running the studio, but I heard it was just fierce. She was very demanding and had high expectations for all her students. It was a requirement that you brought your A game whenever you stepped onto her stage. It was a total dictatorship; and as a result, she produced some incredible artists. Tony was BJ's, as she was affectionately called, caregiver and a close family member. He knew what she would have wanted; and as a result, we had some of the best teachers in front of us.

We were learning, taking classes with a teacher that was also an instructor at Alvin Ailey; Tina Bush taught us the Horton Technique. The great Shirley Black Brown taught us Graham Technique. Buster Grant taught us the Limón Technique & Jazz, David Robinson Michael Peter's assistant choreographer and the person I most admired and wanted to be like on stage taught us jazz/modern. Our African dance teachers were from Africa. And I was loving everything I was learning. The more flexible I was getting; I was including it into my show. I would take two chairs put them together, then stand up on them, push the chairs a part into a full spilt then bring the chairs back together again. People were coming to me, asking, "My god! What are you doing stripping? I mean, you have natural talent as a dancer."

Little did they know, I was in dance school, and everything I was learning in dance school, I was putting in my performances. I had fans on both the male and female circuits. Broadway actors, dancers, producers, and music artists. Little did they know, I was going to school taking 14 to 20 classes a week. I was definitely utilizing everything I learned. I realized it wasn't enough. I came to this realization while in Los Angeles.

This was at a time when I was on tour with Mozell Entertainment Group with the play, "Middle-Class Black Folk in the Claire De Lune," which was getting a lot of interest and heat at the time. We had a meeting with a major cable network and a major agency. The cable network told Richard, who wrote the play, "We loved the script, fire all the actors." Then, we were about to audition for a major agency. A girl in the office saw me and said, "You're Sir Lancelot." I said, "Yes, I am." and she said, "You're one of those exotic dancers in New York." I said, "Yes, I am." and she said, "Ugh!" and walked away, that was the first time I had ever experienced anybody, at least in my face, have a negative reaction towards exotic dancing. It took me for a loop. The cable network said to fire all the actors, and now I was about to audition for an agency all the way in LA, which, by the way, didn't go well. Someone in the office where I was auditioning already had a negative opinion of me. This was when I realized that everyone wasn't seeing exotic dancers the way I was seeing it in my head; and, as an actor, I may have needed a whole lot more work on my craft.

They Haven't Made An AX That Can Chop Down A Dream

The second time I had an epiphany was when there was a major event happening in NY. A well-known dancer was being honored for their fifty years in show business. I knew the producer of the event and a few of the people that would be attending the event, yet I wasn't invited. That, to me, was a loud and clear statement that I was just seen as an exotic dancer, nothing more, and nothing less. I knew Broadway actors, singers, choreographers, and music producers. I envisioned myself being seen on that level, but I wasn't, and needed that wake-up call. I was a bit delusional. Just because people knew my name, or enjoyed my performance as an exotic dancer, it didn't mean that I was seen as an artist on the same level as the people I was coming across, nor should I have been.

Your ego can sometimes play tricks on you. There was much more work, sacrifice, and commitment needed in order to be respected at that level. There was one person in particular whose mere presence had convinced me it was time to part ways with exotic dance. Being a part of the Red Bone Dancers had exposed me to different people in the industry. This one particular person came down to clean up some of our dances. His personality, to me, was bigger than life. He stood at 6 foot 7 and had this deep voice. I knew about him from the 7-up commercials; I had no idea of his resume. Geoffrey Holder was an incredible dancer/choreographer; he directed "The Wiz" on Broadway; he directed and choreographed "Timbuktu" on Broadway and was also an actor.

His well-known movie credit was James Bond's "Live and let die." He was very well known in the theater community and dance world. I'm sitting here having lunch with Geoffrey Holder; he would come down and clean up Frank's choreography. He didn't look like a traditional dancer and choreographer; yet, when I looked him up, he had so many accomplishments as a dancer, actor, choreographer, and director; plus, he was a photographer as well. After meeting him, it became important for me to be an artist; but, more importantly, to be seen and respected as an artist by those same people I was exposed to. I began to realize exotic dancing wasn't the vehicle for that.

At that point, I made the decision to dedicate myself to the craft. No matter how long it took, I was going to keep learning and growing as an artist. I was living with a girl at the time. I left to moved back home, and just went full throttle with Bernice Johnson; I was taking an acting class at Ted Bardy's Acting Studio, and Second City Improvisation in New York City, I was working on plays and studying with Mozell Entertainment Group. "If I'm going to be an artist, and be taken seriously, I have to study my craft."

What Tony knew, that I didn't know at the time, was the probability of me being a trained dancer, with the skill set to dance on Broadway as an ensemble dancer, was not realistic. Being an actor who can dance and has stage presence and technique, in addition to this, a unique ability to tap dance, was much more realistic; but that would take incredible work, sacrifice, and time.

I will never forget; I was faced with a choice… I was in the midst of training at Bernice Johnson. I was traveling and doing gigs in different states. I remember Tony Marlborough was putting a lot of money out for us. And we were getting ready for a big show at the end of the year. This was in our fourth year, and we were technically ready to do this incredible piece called "Embers," choreographed by Fred Benjamin, which is a part of the repertoire of Bernice Johnson. Now, this was the first time we were doing an actual piece that was a part of the legacy of Bernice Johnson. So, Tony wanted us to be ready, and we started from the beginning of the year.

I was only missing class, because I was earning money dancing in different states around the country. After a while, he said, "Listen, you're going to have to make a choice. You're missing too many classes." then I'm like, "Yeah, you can't tell me not to make money. I'm working." he says, "Yeah, but you're going to have to make a choice, because you're missing too many classes." I said, "Well, listen, you're not going to make me make a choice over money, because I'm going to take the money. I have to live." he said, "Well then, okay, take the money. But you can't take the class." I left, and he never called me. He never said, "Please come back." in about a month or so, I missed it so much. I was like, "What the hell was I thinking? I have this incredible opportunity to continue to work on my technique and get better as a dancer, and I'm worried about making these little bits of pennies now." I went back to him and begged him to take me back. And he said, "Absolutely!"

I came back, but lost my spot, even though I had the lead before I left. When I came back, they had given the lead to Brian, who actually deserved it, because he looked great dancing. They had progressed so much within the month, or two, that I was gone. It was incredible. Like I said, we were taking 14 to 20 classes a week. And, within the time period I was gone, two of the guys, Brian Defreitas and Bryce Vick, had just progressed so much. I mean, I was blown away. I was just so happy to be back as a part of this, because this was huge for us. It was like the school recognizing and saying, "You have arrived, in regard to your technique. We are now at a point technique-wise where we are ready to try to perform this piece."

We showcased it at the Apollo, and we did a pretty good job. So, I'm forever grateful to Tony Marlborough for believing in me, but also being strict enough with me to let me know what tough love is like. Either you're going to sacrifice and do this all the way, or not do it at all. It taught me a lot. It taught me about sacrifice and dedication, but it also taught me about setting yourself up for the future.

Don't be so shortsighted trying to make pennies now, and not figure out what you're doing in the future. So now, constantly, I'm thinking about playing chess, not checkers. Making decisions that are setting me up for the next five to ten years. I've learned that from being with Tony, who was like, "Yeah, it's great to make that money, but that ain't helping you down the line." When I made the choice to go full throttle into the arts, I decided that I was going to do whatever it took, however long it took. I knew it wasn't going to be overnight, or easy, because I wasn't young. I had a lot of things that were going to be up against me. I wasn't that traditional-looking person in terms of my body. My competition has been taking classes and studying dance & acting for a large part of their life. So, I made the choice that I was going to stick with it, no matter what it took; simply because I loved it.

That's all that mattered. Twenty years later, I got my first movie, where I was the second lead. It is out on most platforms. It's on about six platforms right now. It just went worldwide. I'm very proud to say the movie "Eddie" is a tribute to the sacrifice, commitment, and the belief that I was going to get that shot, thanks to Fred Sciretta, Artistic Director & founder of Open End Repertory Theater, whom I've studied under and worked with for the last fifteen years. I didn't know when, I didn't know how long, but I knew an opportunity would present itself sooner or later. Just like I didn't know when, or how long it would take to get that shot after being blackballed during my college years. Having that true belief in yourself is a life-altering thing. As a result, I continue to perfect my craft as a tap dancer and actor, and twenty years later, I am able to showcase both talents. I'm forever a part of the films that are live streaming on several platforms around the world.

It's surreal, but it's not bittersweet. It's surreal that this is happening. I'm so happy to have been able to stick it out. There were several other male prospects that came through the program over those four years. The three of us who started the program together, I'm proud to say, graduated and are working artists. Brian Defreitas opened up his own dance studio. He took the dance technique and became a professional ballroom dancer. Then, we've got my man, Bryce Vick, who's a big-time choreographer for Ashanti and several R&B artists. You've seen his work on the Grammys, and other award shows over the years. It's great to be a part of that legacy. I have to give a shout-out, and definitely acknowledge the man that got the ball rolling for me and got me to Bernice Johnson, where I got my scholarship. He gave me the information, walked me down there, and I did the rest.

Frank West is the Executive Director of" Redbone Entertainment." I want to thank him because he got the ball rolling and introduced me to another phase of my life. Oh, I'd be remiss, if I didn't also mention two other males that were a part of the program. They were young kids at the time and already at the studio when I got there; they are Lameek Dean and Anthony Godineaux. We were all in class together. It was this cast of characters, but we were very close and loved each other. Lameek and I still keep in contact. In fact, I produced, wrote, and directed a show years later called "The Journey," which was loosely based on my experience as an adult at BJ's. It touched on the four-year intensive dance program that I went through. You actually experience what I went through taking the classes as an adult with kids. Messing up and not knowing what I was doing, people were frustrated, and fellow classmates were looking at me, annoyed. Then, as you follow him through his journey and transition, he becomes a dancer, because of perseverance and hard work. The whole second half of the show, you'll witness his transformation through this incredible mix of different dance styles and techniques to hip hop music. I chose Lameek for the lead because, ironically, Lameek was there when I was taking the classes. He knew exactly what I was writing about because he was there. He could tell you. I was this big football player, stiff and sweaty, trying to take class. Then, you had Lameek, this little kid who just had all this talent and facility. We were all in class at the same time, and he saw the progress, but he also saw the struggle. So, he was able to play the role from a sense of knowing because he was a part of it.

My four-year intensive at Bernice Johnson would ultimately set me up for the next twenty years; it gave me the foundation I would need to continue to grow a little each day as an artist. It presented me the art of tap that would ignite a fire that burns bright in me and keeps me hungry and passionate about being the best artist I can possibly be—living up to the incredible artist I believe God intended me to be.

Without realizing it at the time, I was following those five keys to success:

1. Being comfortable in your own skin, knowing your worth, and knowing you are worthy of anything your mind can conceive you can achieve.

2. Educating yourself.

3. Surround yourself with people that have done what you're trying to do or who support what you're trying to do.

4. Be willing to put that work in.

5. Truly believe you can achieve.

They Haven't Made An AX That Can Chop Down A Dream

They Haven't Made An AX That Can Chop Down A Dream

They Haven't Made An AX That Can Chop Down A Dream

They Haven't Made An AX That Can Chop Down A Dream

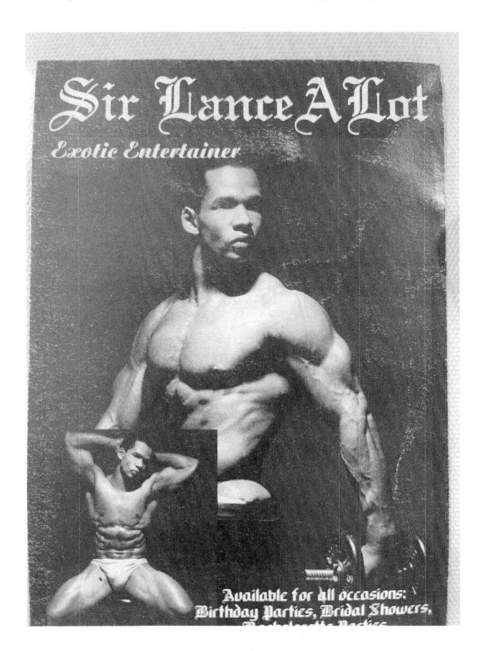

They Haven't Made An AX That Can Chop Down A Dream

They Haven't Made An AX That Can Chop Down A Dream

Chapter 7

Creation Of "T3 Technique" The Theobald Tap Technique

THe next reinvention would be to come up with my own tap technique that I call the 'T3 Technique', which is The Theobald Tap Technique. Now, what's interesting about tap dance is that I didn't want to tap dance. I had gone back to school with a full scholarship at Bernice Johnson dance studio. And, like I said, I took many classes each week. For the first three months, or so, I had a tap class on Saturdays, which was when I used to have dance classes all day. I didn't really want to tap dance. I wasn't really interested in it, because I had taken it in the summer and it was really difficult for me; but Tony Marlborough insisted that I tap dance.

Months later, I think it had to have been three months, he kept telling me, "You need to go and take the class. Why aren't you in class?" I answered, "I don't eat all day, and that's the hour I take off to get something to eat." Ofcourse all I was doing was making excuses. He kept getting on me, to the point where he came to me and said, "I'm going to take your scholarship away from you, unless you go and take tap class." he said, "This, son, is going to be the one thing that separates you from everybody else. That'll be the thing that's going to make you special."

And so, I went in there, I took one tap class, and I was hooked—I mean hooked. Loved it. And you got to know, again, with my personality, anything that I start to set my mind to, anything I do, I approach with a certain pathos, energy and focus. I had one class, and then just fell in love with tap dance. It was partly due to a teacher by the name of Rashamella Cumbo, who was one of the stars of 'Black and Blue' that was on Broadway. She was one of my teachers, and she could see right away that I had a passion for tap. So much so, that she taught a younger female dancer and myself a modified version of the famous Mr. Bojangles & Shirley Temple stair tap dance routine in my first year.

It became an obsession with me. I was tap dancing underneath the table at dinner. I was tap dancing while walking down the street. I was tap dancing in the house, making all kinds of noise. My thing with my students now is, "If somebody—your parents, or your husband, or wife, is not telling you to stop, you're driving me crazy; stop all that noise, then you know tap dancing is not your passion." Many tap dancers I know have heard that statement, or something similar to that many times. Especially for myself, it would drive my girlfriend at the time, now my wife, absolutely bananas because I would tap dance as she was talking to me. She would say, "Are you paying attention to me?" I would tap dance as we're eating underneath the table. I'd be practicing paradiddles.

They Haven't Made An AX That Can Chop Down A Dream

And don't get me started, when I was in a grocery store, it was just carte blanche—the wide open space with the carts was like my personal stage. I'd be making all kinds of tap dance noise, jumping up and down, clicking my heels together. And my wife was like, "Would you act like a doggone adult and stop acting like a child?" but she didn't understand that fervor. Tap dance had just swept me away to the point where I used to think about it every single day, creating rhythms every single day. And it just became my passion.

Being called stupid by a nine-year-old child for not understanding how to execute a step, lit a fire in me that made me hungry to learn, partly because I was determined not to be called stupid again by a nine-year-old. I was soaking up years of tap dance in months because I was just so focused and zealous.

What also happened was being in class with kids who had been tap dancing since they were three and four years old. I learned to gather learned information and interpret it in such a way that later on, it would help benefit others, such as myself, who would learn to tap dance at a later age.

One of the other things in my favor, was that I was surrounded by some of the best tap dancers, as well as some of the best teachers in the world. They were coming through Bernice Johnson, because Bernice Johnson was a very famous dance school.

I'll give you an example. When I took tap in the summer, my first tap teacher was a guy by the name of Tarik Winston. He was in the show River

They Haven't Made An AX That Can Chop Down A Dream

Dance, the original production. You can look it up right now. It's on video. He's one of the guys that traded taps with the river dance duo. He ran up the wall and did a flip on the wall backwards in tap shoes; it was an incredible moment captured on video!

He was my first tap teacher, and we became pretty cool with one another. He was an excellent tap dancer but, in terms of a teacher, he scared me. I had never seen tap before; he right away started doing a combination, and then said, "Okay, you guys do it." I just had no idea even where to start. That was the real reason why it actually took me three months to get up enough courage to take a tap class. He really was a great guy, though.

I was then blessed to have Roosevelt Nettles, who also became a teacher and another friend of mine, thanks to Bernice Johnson. These were all the people who were just feeding me just incredible information on how to tap dance. I was sucking it up. When I tell you focused, I was razor focused. To the point where Roosevelt started training me personally at a studio in Harlem called the Harlem Y.M.C.A. I used to drive up there twice a week to take tap classes with him at the Harlem Y. I learned a great deal hanging out and tap dancing with Roosevelt Nettles.

The one person who really changed my life in terms of truly helping me to create, understand and break down tap dance was a guy by the name of Ted Levy. We are friends, even today, however, I call him my mentor. He was the one who really made me understand and break it down in a way in which I started to discern how to construct rhythms, and also how to control my sounds. That was the key. He was the first person to really teach me how to control every sound. He also taught me how important every sound is, and that we are musicians. Under his tutelage, I learned that whatever you could do with your hands, you can do with your feet.

Once he opened that door, it never closed. I began to just focus on mastering everything, especially the fundamentals. I used to study with him, and we use to trade-off. I would train him and teach him how to eat right. I would train him with physical fitness exercises; and then, he would train me with tap movements and combinations. I started taking his tap class at American Dance & Drama in Queens. Then, I started taking a class from him at a legendary dance studio called Fazils, located at 743 8th avenue between 46th & 47th in NYC. After seventy-three years, this landmark dance studio closed its doors in 2008.

Many of the famous old-timers would make appearances during Ted's tap class. It was just an amazing experience. Savion Glover would come through often because he and Ted Levy were good friends. Savion would have rehearsal on the second floor, right above our class. Ted Levy also helped Savion clean the Broadway show, "Bring in da Noise Bring in da Funk." Ted Levy also was the choreographer for Gregory Hines when he won his Tony in "Jelly's Last Jam". Needless to say, I'm talking about an incredible teacher in Ted Levy, but also a wealth of information.

I learned I was also a part of a lineage that made it even more special. The knowledge, techniques, and some of the rhythms that I learned were passed on from the beginnings of tap dance, or juba dance.

They Haven't Made An AX That Can Chop Down A Dream

Tap dance evolved: after the Stono Rebellion in 1739, plantation owners began to fear that enslaved people were hiding secret codes in their drumming patterns. So, they took their drums from them. Instead of using drums, the enslaved people used their bodies & feet to communicate and to make music to accompany their singing and dancing. This American musical tradition became known as "Pattin Juba," and it was the main accompaniment to the American folk dance known as juba dance which evolved into tap dance. Master juba dancer, William Henry Lane, became well known in the minstrel's shows. He influenced the development of modern tap dance.

Now you have to think, how special is it to realize that you're learning technique and movements connected to a lineage back to the enslaved Africans called Juba Dance? This was possible because I learned from Ted Levy, who learned from Sammy Davis Jr.'s manager, who was also connected and influenced by Gregory Hines, Jimmy Slyde, The Nicholas Brothers, and Sammy Davis Jr. The latter was influenced by his dad and uncle who he performed with on the Vaudeville circuit when he was three years old. Davis had studied under Bill "Bojangles" Robinson, who got his start on the vaudeville circuit in the early 1900s. He was influenced by the creator of tap dance Willian Henry Lane who had become known as the best dancer on the minstrel circuit in the 1840s, after beating the favorite white dancer in that period. You see how it's connected all the way to the beginnings of tap dance from the juba dance. To me, that was something special.

I was a part of this rare family, this unique brotherhood of tap dance knowledge. I am now passing it on to the people that I am teaching. I take that history extremely seriously. For years, I would not teach tap dance, especially in certain dance schools, because there were things I would notice with hip hop, the lack of discipline that sometimes surfaced with kids who were taking hip hop, especially the kids I was teaching. It was very clear to me that tap dance was my passion. I realized early on that I only wanted those students who were serious about learning tap. I was there to share invaluable information and technique.

I adopted a philosophy, 'if you're here other than to tap dance and learn this incredible art form, do not take my class.' I've stopped teaching certain classes, because that's how much respect I have for the art form and the knowledge that had been passed down to me from the motherland. I could be delusional, but that's how I saw it, that's exactly how I still approach it. It didn't matter what level you were as a tap dancer, or whether you could tap dance at all; it did matter that you were there to learn. I never meant for it to appear to be mean; it's just that tap dance had ignited such a burning fire in me, and I have so much love and respect for the art form.

I continue to study my craft and create rhythms, so that when I teach those individuals that take my class, I'm giving my heart to them, but at the same time, I'm also receiving. As I was passionately teaching them how to separate their sounds, teaching them different rhythms, and teaching them body control, I was also making myself better as a teacher, and as a tap dancer, and the students were also getting better and growing as tap dancers. It's a win-win.

A former student came to me recently and reminded me of something I said to her years ago that has stuck with her ever since. I asked, "What was that?" She said, I looked at her and said, "Don't worry, I don't need the best dancer; I need the hardest worker, because I can make the hardest worker into the best dancer." Ironically in her senior year, she became my dance captain in a show I produced called, "The Journey."

:

A few years ago, a young lady wound up being my dance partner. I started teaching her; she had been taking tap since she was a little kid and loved it. She took a class and started using words like, "You're brilliant. Some of these rhythms are really, really good." as a result, after a few classes, she started taking classes with me privately. By me giving my all as her instructor, including the knowledge I had, I was also receiving, because I was getting better and better.

My rhythms were getting better and tighter, plus I continued to emphasize fundamentals, technique, body control and shifting of your weight. I began to become more specific with my technique in my other tap classes as well. I started emphasizing to watch, not just what my feet were doing, but watch exactly what my entire body was doing. She gave me the idea of naming my own technique. I eventually came up with "T3 Technique" (The Theobald Tap Technique). I had learned as an adult, and I was learning at such a rapid pace. I was with kids that were much better than I was in the beginning, and in order for me to catch up, I had to learn little ways of interpreting what the teacher was doing.

I started watching their movements more closely, the shifting of weight, and watching certain things one does naturally without thinking. Ultimately, as I was trying so hard to be the best that I could be, I started coming up with these different ways of understanding the technique. Then, as I taught other people, I could teach them, understanding the issues they were having, especially adults. I had some of the same issues also, as I was learning and understanding the technical aspect of tap dance. I sometimes understood why students were having a difficult time, because I was having a difficult time when I started. I always say, "Trust the process, and enjoy the journey of learning." Enjoy the process from not knowing, to the point of knowing; enjoy the entire journey in between. When you can do that, then the process of learning becomes exhilarating and fun. It's akin to being a kid in a candy store for the first time. All it takes is for a person to switch their mindset. I always say there is your third eye looking down on you, judging you, while you are learning and doing, criticizing what you look like, wondering what other people are thinking about you. You may internalize that third eye, asking, "Are they making fun of me because I can't get it? Oh god, I'm the worst in the class!" These are things you are doing to yourself. Get rid of that third eye, and you'll open yourself up to happiness, joy, and fulfillment, because that's what the arts can bring to you.

They Haven't Made An AX That Can Chop Down A Dream

Just a simple tweak of the mindset, and students were learning at a rapid pace; and then, you had people who were taking the class for maybe two or three years with me, and they were killing it. I've had students that have gone on to college to be the president of their tap club in college. I've had kids go on to be professional tap dancers. The list goes on, the people that I've been able to affect; but, it was because of T3 Technique that I had never named and never even thought about, until one of my students, Tali Tadmor, said, "Your technique, the way you teach it, it makes it so much easier to understand." so that's how T3 Technique was born.

Now, every time I teach any private students, or anytime that I teach a class, I do a half hour of T3 Technique and I'll say: "What's the name of this technique? T3 Technique. What does that stand for? The Theobald Tap Technique." this is something that will be my legacy, because I'm going to continue to teach it. There are dancers who have come through my classes and have gone on to teach. I have some students who are still tap dancing, and others that have gone on to be professional tap dancers. One of my favorite students trained with me and became part of the Tony Award-winning musical "Billy Elliot." Another student landed the best friend role in "Billy Elliot," which was a major tap dance role, but decided to do the show "Mary Poppins" instead.

To say the least, it's been a pleasure to watch kids come through me and blossom. I firmly believe it was because of me giving my all and giving them everything I had as a teacher. I also was receiving more than I was giving, because I was getting better as a dancer too, which was making them better.

I was becoming more precise with my rhythms. I became a musician. I always say, "Whatever you can do with your hands, you can do with your feet." I'll always emphasize that 'learning to separate your sounds and learning to control each sound is paramount'.

The concept of "No breath, no life" was something that Ted Levy taught me. What he meant by that is you have to breathe into your rhythm. When I say breathe, that means to lift your feet up and legs up. Many students come to me, and they know shuffles, they know flaps, but can you control your shuffles? Can you control your flaps? That's a completely different thing, the ability to place that sound exactly where you want it, time and time again. Shuffles are two sounds, but people may often see them as one movement when in actuality, its two separate sounds: distinct sounds with their own universe. And that's how I teach it.

This is why my students can go on, and they can take a class with anybody, because they understand their fundamentals. Like in ballet, you have your fundamentals. Tap, you have your fundamentals. Like in sports, you have your fundamentals. Basketball players, you can be as fancy as you want to be, but you better understand and constantly work on your fundamentals. And that's how T3 Technique was born.

Little did I know that was a talent that God had instilled and given to me since I was probably younger, but I had never really blossomed, or worked on that talent until I got older. When I started getting into tap, I realized that I had the ability to create rhythms. I could do it so freely, I thought everybody was able to do that. We were in the studio one afternoon hitting a combination, and a student stopped and said, "Man, I wish I could create the rhythms like that." and I'm like, "All you got to do is just hear the rhythm and create the beat with your feet." she says, "Yeah, it just doesn't come to me like that. I can tap dance and if you give me the rhythm, I can duplicate it. But to create rhythms from the top of your head is such a blessing. It's such a talent."

I had no idea. I would hear the music. I could hear the sounds in my head, and I would just create these sounds and create these rhythms; I could just do it all day long. One of the fascinating things about being an artist is that freedom to create, that excitement to create, that giving and taking. Again, the more I give to my students, the more I receive because, the better I get at delivering, the better they get at receiving. This is because they are giving me back the energy I'm giving out. I had an incredible full circle bucket list moment thanks to my former student, now dance partner. I was presented with an opportunity to tap dance with a band called "The Fellowship"? At the Roosevelt Public Library Theatre, for black history month. I've tap danced in movies, on TV, and in videos, but the one thing I hadn't done was tap dance with a seven-piece band. It was a bucket list item for me because all the tap dancers I watched footage of, studied, and had a connection to, had performed with bands, or orchestras. It was a full-circle moment that had me so excited that I was too amped to be nervous, which is what I should have felt. I had never performed with a band before, didn't know what to expect, and had one rehearsal to get it right. It was such an incredible feeling to be able to do one rehearsal with "The Fellowship" band and become an additional instrument. It was a surreal moment I shall never forget. For two decades I had spent hours upon hours in dance studios, to the point where I thought I was going to have to have a knee operation. Endless hours, pounding on that dance floor, creating countless rhythms and combinations that were pouring out of me like sweat after a good workout, but that's what being passionate about something really is all about. Those years of grinding, prepared me for that night. By the time I got the chance to work with "The Fellowship," and Long Island Music and Entertainment Hall of Fame recipient: Dr. Francis Abel legendary Rhythm & Blues artist. I was more than ready to fly like a bird, soaring in the beautiful blue sky.

Following those "Five keys" had prepared me for that moment. By knowing my worth, being comfortable about who I was, knowing that I was worthy of anything that I dreamed of, but also understanding that all the potential to be what I wanted to be was up to me. It was locked inside of me. All I had to do was just let it out. I was more than ready; I was prepared, and I was surrounded by other incredible artists. As a result, the night was magical and entertaining, and the audience loved it. Being willing to put that work in, year in and year out and believing I can achieve, led me to a night of ease, grace and spontaneous creativity.

I have to thank Bernice Johnson from the bottom of my heart, especially Tony Marlborough, for, first of all, recognizing that this would be the thing that would separate me and make me special. It is and it has been. I'm also grateful the studio was the vehicle providing the lessons, spending the money, and putting the best teachers in front of me, who gave me the information and foundation. I know you can have all the potential in the world, but if you don't have that information, and you don't have that education and the proper teachers, there's only so far you can go.

I was blessed to have some of the best, some of the greatest teachers, who were connected to that lineage, that tap dance knowledge, which was kindred to the beginning.

One of the things that I thoroughly enjoy is when I watch my private students come in; they're small, young, shy and with little confidence. And then you watch them grow over the years. They just blossom into confident dancers, but also confident individuals. I think one of the things that gets overlooked a lot of times is that people need something to be good at, to thrive at, that gives them the conviction to walk out there, holding their head high, knowing that they're good at something, that they can do something that others can't.

I've seen tap dance enhance people's lives, build their self-esteem, and augment their confidence. I've watched students; I've taught who started off shy and timid, and then have grown into this confident, self-assured dancer that transfers over into their everyday life. It's wonderful to witness growth as a tap dancer, to see all the information they have been given over the years, and all the techniques they now have.

To watch students hit complicated rhythms with precision and clarity is rewarding, but to watch students be able to gain confidence, become more self-assured and walk with their heads held high because of the tap is a blessing.

A friend of mine brought her daughter to me, because she felt she wasn't growing as a tap dancer and thought T3 Technique was what she needed to get better. I was honored because I believe that this technique can enhance people's lives in the positive, in ways such as teaching them how to have something that they can call their own, that they can be good at, that they can show the world that, 'hey, I am something, and I am somebody; I am a tap dancing musician.'

I think one of the things I would love to do and will do is teach the T3 Technique to tap dancers all over the country. I plan to have this legacy of dancers that know my technique and understand the lineage of how this technique is connected to history in America. I think it's important to understand that this technique is an outgrowth from the beginning years in the 19th century, where tap dance evolved from the juba dance. And to me, that is so powerful. That's such an honor.

I have so much respect for the people who taught me, like Ted Levy, Rashamella Cumbo, and the late Roosevelt Nettle. As a result, I have an expectation for my students who come to learn, to suck up the information I'm giving them, and work at their craft.

I would love to be able to teach this technique around the country, because tap dance is an important part of American culture as well as American history. Tap dance is the first dance form that originated in America. That's right. It may not be as popular as hip-hop dance, which also originated in America, but it is still the only dance form that is both visual and audio. It's still a unique dance form that many people can't do, which makes those that can teach/dance and create a commodity. This is exactly what Tony Marlborough said years ago. He said, "This is going to be the thing that is going to separate you. This is going to be the thing that is going to make you special." and for damn sure, it is. Big shout-out to Tony Marlborough. Big shout-out to Bernice Johnson. And a big shout-out to the late, great Roosevelt Nettles, who passed on a couple of years ago. To my mentor, who I continue to have nothing but the utmost respect for, Ted Levy. I love you, man. Peace.

They Haven't Made An AX That Can Chop Down A Dream

They Haven't Made An AX That Can Chop Down A Dream

Chapter 8

Doing God's Work "Philanthropy"

Next, stop philanthropic and activist work. Since I was seventeen years old, I believed that I had a larger purpose in life. When you really truly believe that in your core, you start to do things that exemplify that feeling. You have a sense of compassion, purpose, dignity, and sensitivity toward others.

I have always felt that I was here on earth to do God's work. My goal is to be a beacon of positive change to the human condition. I'd always thought I would get visibility from playing football, a possible platform to affect people in a positive way. When things didn't quite work out the way I imagined, years went by, as I continued on my journey of self-reinvention. That feeling of my ultimate purpose has never strayed too far from my mind. I was constantly waiting, until I achieved a certain level, to then be able to use that status to help others.

I started feeling as though I needed to do something now; continuing to wait until the so-called right time was no longer an option.

One of the things I started doing, every chance I got, was talk to kids. For example, if somebody wanted me to come speak to their students on a career day, I would do it, no questions asked. I went back and spoke at my high school. I did several of those sessions where I'd go to individual classes and talk. I went to at-risk schools and spoke to kids about my transition from football to dance. I also shared how I got kicked out of two different schools, and then how I never let that define me. In addition to high schools, I went to grammar schools and spoke. My sister is a special education grammar school teacher, and I've spoken to her class. I was asked to be on a panel for a middle school that spoke about different career choices. My god sister asked me to come down and talk to her students on career day in Brownsville, which is a hardcore part of Brooklyn, New York.

I was very excited about being able to talk to young, urban, mostly African American and Latin American kids in Brooklyn, because I grew up in Brooklyn. I did their career day four years in a row. I remember the first year, my dad and I came down. I had this pivotal moment. I'm in this class, and the students were listening to me talk. And this one girl said, "Excuse me, sir, can you do me a favor?" Now, these kids are no more than ten or eleven years old. She says to me in a serious voice, "Can you please talk to my friend? You know he is always wearing his pants down to his knees." That caught me off guard because, one, I wasn't expecting that, and two, that was considered a style in urban areas.

The kid she was referencing, was sitting there with his pants literally down by his thighs. I guess a higher power took over and started talking for me. I said I understood him because he and I are a lot alike. I asked, "What's your name?" He told me his name. Then I said, "You and I are very similar." He sat up, signaling that I had his attention. I then said, "You and I both want to be seen, recognized, and acknowledged for the unique and special person that we know that we are." I also added, "Of course, you're special; I can see that, you know it, and you want others to see it and recognize it as well. And right now, wearing your pants down to your knees is your way of saying look at me, acknowledge me. You're crying out for people to say, hey, that's…" I continued, "You don't have to do it by wearing your pants down to your knees." He sat up straighter and started not just listening; he started hearing me. I said, "Everybody has a talent that God gives them. Trust me, everybody does. Sometimes it is not obvious to some of us, but God gives every one of us talents—sometimes several, sometimes they're more obvious than others." Then I asked, "What's your talent?" He said, "I don't have no talents." Then he said, "I know how to talk to girls," and everybody started laughing. I said, "Come on, you got to have some kind of talent." Now, I had never done, or said this before. In my mind, I was like, what if he really doesn't have any obvious talents? Then the girl who initiated everything says, "Show him your book." He was very hesitant. After a moment, he goes to a desk, pulls out this book, and then hands it to me. To my joyous surprise, inside this book are these incredible drawings of superheroes that he had made up. I mean, remarkable! I looked at it hiding tears in my eyes and said, "You know, there are parents that will pay thousands of dollars for their kid to learn how to do what you do naturally. This right here, is a God-given talent I was talking about. You need to work on this, and continue to work on this, because this is the kind of talent, I was telling you about, this is what makes you unique, this is what makes you stand out." He sat there and listened to me; it felt like I had gotten through to him. I continued talking to the whole class, because now I had a platform to use. I said, "You guys are all gifts from God made in his image, and don't let anyone try to convince you that you aren't." We continued our discussion and discovered that many of the kids in this class were multi-talented. You had some kids that could play several different instruments or had strength in a sport (or two), there were clothing designers, and may I remind you, these kids were only ten and eleven years old. That was a spectacular day that ended with the school band playing, and they were phenomenal! Then come to find out, I saw a lot of the kids in that class were in the band as well.

I realized these kids were talented. This concept became a theme over the years—find your talent, and understand you are just as good as anybody else. I wanted them to know we are all children of God, and he loves us equally. I did a whole presentation one year with that same school on anti-bullying. I explained to the kids that bullies are very insecure themselves, and that they're usually being bullied at home, or somewhere else. I did all kinds of stuff with them, and it was just a phenomenal experience during those four years. I got a call in the fourth year from Yvette, my god sister, and she said, "Lance, I have a question I need to ask you. Would you like to be the keynote speaker at our school's graduation?" I was surprised—to say the least. They believed the kids would want me to be the keynote speaker of their graduation. That blew me away, bringing tears to my eyes. Being asked to be the keynote speaker of their graduation was a testament to the fact that I was doing God's work and they were hearing me. I answered, "Absolutely!" I will always remember the theme of my keynote speech. It was based on the talent(s) that parents would pay thousands of dollars for their kids to learn how to do. And these kids had it naturally. My theme was, "Parents, support your kids."

Parents support the talents of their kids; sometimes the youngsters are multi-talented. They should be encouraged, whatever it takes, to get them into these programs. As I was talking, I distinctly remember that many parents had this undertone, whispering, at the same time. Then, it hit me—remember, I was an exotic dancer. One of the places I performed & was very popular in was Brooklyn, New York. I knew this funny feeling might have been connected to murmurs—and I decided to deal with it. I stopped what I was saying to address the elephant that was obviously in the room. I announced to all the ladies who were trying to figure it out, confirming that I was indeed 'Sir Lancelot.' "Yes, I am. Yes. I used to be an exotic dancer." All of a sudden, you see ladies breaking out into a chatter. Once addressed, I had their undivided attention. I continued, "I am him, and now I'm standing here doing my thing as the keynote speaker of your kid's graduation."

That was an incredible experience, all the way around. To know that you affected these kids enough to be asked to be their keynote speaker, was an awesome feeling. And that transition, to being a motivational speaker, just continued to help me delve into my philanthropic work. I knew that this was the path I was supposed to be on with direction from my higher power.

My next step was to use my talents to help make a change. I learned so much being a part of Mozell Entertainment Group, with regard to producing and directing. I was a choreographer, dancer, and actor. I decided to make good use of my skill set and created/produced a show called Hip Hop Fusion. Hip Hop Fusion was a showcase where I combined several different dance styles with hip-hop dance, using hip-hop music. At the time, it was fresh, new and hadn't been done before, especially in that area. I would blend hip hop with ballet, hip hop with modern, hip hop with jazz, hip hop with Irish step dance and hip hop with flamenco dance.

It was a ninety-minute showcase. Among the performers were friends and artists that I had been working with, who were singers, comedians, and rappers. Initially, it was with dancers who had marginal, talent; but what they did have was a commitment to be the best they could possibly be. I disciplined them, taught them, and I took these kids to another level. We would have class twice a week. And then, on the weekend, we'd have seven-hour rehearsals. Okay—that was unheard of in those years, especially since they were not professionals, but I demanded the seven-hour rehearsal. Plus, if you missed more than two rehearsals without explanation, you were off the team. And I had to kick a few people off the team throughout the four years. In addition, lateness meant you had to give me a dollar. I had already taught them that 'early' was on time, being on time was late, and being late was unacceptable—a concept I learned the hard way many years before.

And where did I learn that message? From back in the days when I used to be a football player. I didn't understand it then, but now it was coming around full circle. It was fascinating to watch these kids evolve over the years. At 10 minutes before 12 noon, when rehearsal started, they would be sprinting up the stairs, running, trying to be early knowing that meant being on time. If they were one second late, they owed me money; that practice taught them discipline. And, for the next four years, I produced this show.

Based on past experience, I encouraged each of the 20-25 dancers to sell one ticket to at least 10 family members, that's 10 tickets each. If successful, you then have yourself, a nice, chunk of money. Many times, we were able to exceed our goal in ticket sales. In addition, we sold ads to be displayed in the show programs. The first year, I decided to donate some of the proceeds to three different organizations. I'm not going to list the names of the organizations; because it's not about the organizations; it's about giving back to the community. There's also the fact that none of those organizations ever said, 'Thank you'. In fact, I think two of the organizations never even came to see the show. They just graciously accepted the money. Afterwards, I felt a certain kind of way. I said, 'From now on, I'm picking an organization that I truly like, and want to support. I had a project manager who was my left hand (wo)man, Carmen Bazzini. She had a friend who was on the board of the Bethany house. I took it upon myself to go visit the organization, to decide if I was willing to support it. I fell in love as soon as I walked into the building. The Bethany House is a homeless shelter for women, and women with children. Being very familiar with the shelter system in NYC, which I've seen it up close, it can be a scary place. That was a reality, back in the 80's when my father was an officer.

Prior to the visit, I was preparing myself to see something similar to what I remembered. I was pleasantly surprised to find that it was nothing like what I anticipated, at all. In fact, as soon as I walked up to the address, I noticed it was a beautiful house in a quiet neighborhood, and when I walked in, it wasn't just a house; it was truly a home. It was filled with love, warmth, compassion, and concern, and it was clean. The women and children inside the residence were called 'guests;' they were delightful and appreciative of the fact that the Bethany House had taken them in. They were also grateful to the Bethany House for providing basic needs to them. I decided that this was the organization I was going to support financially.

So, the first year, we gave them a portion of our proceeds from the door. I did a video montage, showing where I actually went to the Bethany House and recorded a few of the guests who were sharing about what the Bethany House had done for them. Once again, my experiences with Mozell Entertainment Group had prepared me for what to do.

Gabby, Carmen's daughter, who was my dance captain for two years, helped me put the video together by editing the footage. Then, we added background music, 'Man In The Mirror,' by the late Michael Jackson. The lyrics express the fact that if you want to make any change in the world, start with yourself. Look in the mirror and start the change in yourself; be the change you're looking for. It was so emotional for me. I started crying when I first put it together, and we showed it at the event. We had a table for the guests to donate cash or checks at the end of the night. Fortunately, we were in an area where people wanted, and had the means, to help monetarily.

By the end of the event, we had written a check for $10,000. That's right! Plus, we raised money for the Bethany House over the next three years. Sister Aimee, the founder of the Bethany House, asked me to be a part of their Board of Directors after the fourth year. I had no idea what a Board of Directors even was at the time, but as far as I was concerned, it seemed like one of God's apostles asking me, so I said, "Absolutely!" I soon found out I was in the company of lawyers, accountants, professors, philanthropists, business owners, etc.

It took me a little while to get used to it, but I always had the confidence of Sister Aimee. She was a magnificent fundraiser, and an incredible person in general. I mean, she founded the Bethany House just to help and house women, and women with children. She was masterful at fundraising. Bethany House would give these first-class fundraising events, and Sister Aimee would always have me sit right next to her. I'm telling you, people use to bend over backward to just get to her, to shake her hand, because she was a God-like person. She was a woman of the cloth. To top it off, she was a lot of fun to hang out with. Such a wonderful, wonderful person who saw something in me that I hadn't necessarily seen in myself, yet.

As a result, I've spent the last fifteen years with the Bethany house. It has taught me that becoming homeless is life altering—a major trauma, like PTSD, domestic violence, or, to a lesser extent, this covid 19 pandemic. We must fix what is broken on the inside. First deal with the emotional and mental effects of homelessness through counseling; that's the key. Another component is to provide the necessary resources, educational programs, financial assistance, and work development programs that will prepare individuals to be able to never set foot back in the shelter system again. I helped implement a cultural arts program in 2023 at Bethany House because I knew from experience, the arts can provide humor, happiness and help towards, healing. The first event was held at the Dr. Francis Abel Theatre courtesy of the Roosevelt Public Library located in Roosevelt Long Island. This was a benefit performance of a show I produced called: "Relationships" which was three one act plays about the different stages in male and female relationships. The successful evening brought awareness and support for this new cultural arts program and the special guests that evening were the beautiful ladies of the Bethany House. We combined it with a cultural foods initiative courtesy of the Wayne Gibson Family who donated Jamaican cuisine. The collaboration of all the different components made the launching of this program an incredible success and a blue print for the future.

The world would shut down and we were forcefully introduced to the covid 19 pandemic, I started getting depressed and anxious. It was devastating when we first got locked down, I didn't know what was going on. For the first time, I didn't feel in control; I wasn't able to come out of the house, they closed my gym, and the pandemic took my refuge from me, my therapy. I'd never taken off more than a week, in all the years I've been training, and that's thirty plus years. I found myself wondering how I was going to make money and pay the mortgage. I wasn't sleeping, I began having breathing issues, chest tightness, and then, the whole thing with George Floyd happened. With all that happening at the same time, it just started sparking a lot of emotions that were unconsciously buried inside of me. I've had several run-ins with cops, as a black man in America, living in the inner city of New York. Growing up, I didn't know too many kids in my neighborhood who hadn't had a run-in with the police, at least once, if not more.

All of that was affecting me. I needed to do something to get out of my funk; so, instead of medicating myself, or drinking, I just started doing pushups. I have a gym in my garage. I took it upon myself to just start doing push-ups, pull-ups, chin-ups, dips, and curls. I started feeling a little better. Before you knew it, in the month of May, I had done 10,000 pushups. Now I hadn't talked to my group, Momz-N-Da Hood, since the pandemic started.

Momz-N- Da Hood is a group I created, the first in the world of its kind—break dancing/hip hop dancing mothers in their 50s and 60s. I got a call from them to see how I was doing. They also had been very upset about the George Floyd situation. This was the first time, in all the years we've been together, twenty-one years to be exact, that we were openly discussing black and white race relations, and police brutality.

I said, "You know what, to be honest with you all, hey, this has been going on for years. This is nothing new. I'm not really that affected by it," although, I truly was, because I said, "We know the cops are going to get off, and that's just how it is." Despite the fact that this was next level brutality, I added, "This stuff is embedded in the DNA of America." The ladies were really upset about it. I think the pandemic slowed everyone down enough for them to really see what was going on. In the past, people were so busy with the hustle and bustle of their own lives, I think they weren't really paying attention to what was really going on right underneath their noses. For the first time, we were having a real conversation about what was happening in America. I continued the conversation, "Yes, it is happening. It's been happening, and it's happened to me." I also told them that I was doing these push-ups as a way of taking back control of my life.

I did another 5,000 pushups in the month of June. And they were like, "You know, Lance, you should do something with this; this is phenomenal. You just did 15,000 push-ups, that's amazing!" I got to thinking more about it and agreed, then we plotted. My wife came up with the name, "Push-Up For Your Life" campaign. We then put this push-up show together where I would do the pushups live on Facebook and Instagram; and Barbara, one of the Momz, would host it. Then Sue, and some of the other Momz-N-Da Hood members, Susan, and Wilma, would do the counting and play instruments. It became this show. And "Push-Up For Your Life" was born. The first day, people started coming on, and Barbara was doing an excellent job of hosting and engaging with the audience. Then, Susan was doing the counting, which really came in handy, because I kept losing track of how many pushups I was doing. Then, we had the other moms come on down to count, play the instruments, and interact with me while I was doing pushups. Before you knew it, we started getting donations. One donation led to another donation, and more people started coming on to watch. We did it five days a week, and would go live, on three out of those five days. On the days we didn't go live, I would shoot the video anyway, just so you could see that I did the pushups. Then, Barbara would take it home and speed it up on her computer because we felt it would be too boring if you watched me do pushups for a whole hour on video, without Barbara hosting. In the end, an hour-long video was sped up to three minutes of viewing. The whole crew was Barbara Adler, Susan Estep Fisher, Susan Avery, and Wilma Ruiz, who were all members of "Momz-N-Da hood."

My studio is a relatively small space, and we didn't allow more than three people in the studio at one time, during the height of the pandemic. The girls would take turns coming down to do the counting and play music. We made a whole show out of it. By the time it was finished, at the end of July, we had raised $10,800. Next on our agenda was to figure out who to donate to. I originally chose Black Lives Matter because they were on the front lines doing their thing. In the process, one thing I realized was how difficult it was to give away money, especially to an organization like that. We could not get in contact with them. The one thing I was not going to do, was just hand over a $10,800 check without at least being able to verify the authenticity of the organization, shake their hands and tell their representative about the "Push Up For Your Life" campaign. After more thought and research, we started looking at other organizations that Black Lives Matter supported. Barbara helped along with another original member of Momz-N-Da-hood. They both schooled me on 'not for profit' ratings.

All registered non-for-profit organizations have ratings. If you have a four star rating that means all the money being raised is going towards exactly what they say it's going towards. And so, we looked for 4 star rated organizations. We found this organization called EJI, which is the Equal Justice Initiative. I chose the Equal Justice Initiative, because I had already seen a movie with Michael B. Jordan and Jamie Foxx, which was about the work of EJI. The movie is about a lawyer who gives free services to incarcerated individuals who were wrongly convicted and unable to afford proper legal representation.

At first, I had decided to go to Alabama, where their offices were located; but in the midst of a pandemic, that wasn't going to happen. We got in contact with the director of development who I had the opportunity to have a personal conversation with. She explained to me that their organization has been blessed and has been receiving a tremendous amount of donations during this pandemic, and they're so grateful. She was so impressed to hear about "Push Up For Your Life," and how we raised the money. She did do an interview with me, and we actually got a thank you letter from the founder & Executive Director, Bryan Stevenson. While raising all this money, $10,800 for the Equal Justice Initiative, the Bethany House, because of the pandemic, became financially challenging. Up until the pandemic, when I was actually raising the money for EJI, the Bethany House was in great shape, but because we had to cancel all of our fundraisers and events for the next two years, suddenly now, the Bethany House organization needed help. Ironically, this is what happens to many of the guests at the Bethany House. One moment you're stable and doing well, and in an instant, a situation—in this case, the pandemic, can occur that's out of your control. The next moment, you can find yourself going from stable to unstable quickly, fast, and in a hurry. Fortunately, the Bethany House has wonderful supporters, donors, staff, board, and committee members who have worked hard to keep Bethany House going during those uncertain times. Many people were not that fortunate.

I had already decided to keep going with the push-ups, but never said anything to anyone. By that time, I had done 25,000, 10,000 in May, 5,000 in June, and 10,000 in July. I kept going and doing pushups, partly because someone sent me a post on Facebook where somebody did a hundred thousand pushups; and me, being the competitive person I am, in my mind, I said, "Now, I'm going to have to do a hundred thousand pushups." I didn't say anything. I just kept going. Then, I got hurt. I started having issues with my shoulders and my elbow. I needed to take time off. I needed a couple of weeks, almost a month, from push-ups, although I kept working out, doing other exercises. You see, as I mentioned earlier, in the thirty years of working out, I've never taken more than a week off from training. I pride myself on that discipline, so I did cardio and core work instead. In September, I started back, but I had to begin slowly.

Before I injured myself, I was doing fifty to a hundred pushups a clip, including incline pushups, balance board pushups, and combo pushups.

After I started to heal, I began with twenty-five regular pushups. I realized that all these different types of push-ups were probably the reason I injured my shoulders and elbow. I gradually moved back up to 50 push-ups a clip, but I had lost about a month in time, because of my injury. I wanted to be finished by my birthday on May 31 of the next year, which was 2021, so instead of a hundred thousand in a year, I changed it to 75,000.

I wasn't just doing push-ups. I was doing sit-ups, crunches, pull-ups, curls, squats, and one-leg squats. I actually finished off with 75,000 pushups and over 30,000 other exercises in combination. So actually, I accomplished the 100,000 mark it just wasn't all push-ups, and I finished it by June 4th; the next year, even though I wanted to finish by May 31st. We wound up choosing June 4th so that we could go live on Facebook, at one of the Bethany House locations. What I did was actually raise $14,000 the second time around for the Bethany House.

I decided to put my muscles where my mouth was and do what I could for Bethany House. In a week and a half, we raised $14,000, and I got to say a big thank you to a dear friend of mine who actually donated $10,000 from her and her husband's foundation. I always knew she was going to donate, because she said she would, but I had no idea it would be that amount. Up until that point, I think we had raised $4,000. I wasn't willing to go back to the same people that had donated during the Equal Justice Initiative campaign, in less than a year. I focused on supporters of the Bethany House. We wound up raising over $14,000 by the time it was all said and done. When you know your worth, and you know that you're worthy of anything your mind conceives, you can achieve. When you educate yourself and surround yourself with people that support what you're trying to do. When vcyou're willing to put that work in, no matter what it is, or how long it takes. When you believe that you can achieve anything you want; this is the kind of positive results that can happen.

As a result of the philanthropic work, as well as all the different ventures I did over the years to help the youth be uplifted, and working hard to make a difference, such as being a keynote speaker, teaching, and using my talents to benefit greater causes, I was given the

"2015 Unsung Hero" award, honored at the "People of Distinction Humanitarian Awards" ceremony at City University in New York City.

They Haven't Made An AX That Can Chop Down A Dream

DENTON AVENUE SCHOOL — DECEMBER 13, 2016

LANCELOT THEOBALD JR.

2015 Unsung Hero: Football Star Turned Dancer, Choreographer, Actor & Humanitarian... AFTER OVERCOMING TRAGEDY

EARLY SUCCESS

Early success as an athlete came easy for Lancelot; as a result he was recruited to play high school Football at Holy Cross in Queens NY. But things seemed to unravel senior year as he involved in a deadly plane crash, while visiting University Of Maine on a football- recruiting weekend. Later that same year he was involved in a train accident, car crash and almost drowned. The incredibly optimistic Lancelot would take the half full approach and take these events as a sign to begin his journey of discovering God's special purpose for him in life.

THE TURN-AROUND

Lancelot continued on his journey and would meet Richard Willis Jr who would provide that spark he was looking for.

Manager and best friend for over 20 years now Richard would change his life by introducing Lancelot to the theatre where he would learn to produce and eventually executive produce plays. He would help Richard start Mozell Entertainment Group, featured on the front cover January 2013 issue of "ENDEE MAGAZINE", www.endeeonline.com that is now based out of Los Angeles California. He

would make the incredible transition from athletics to producing/executive producing to studying Ballet, Modern, Jazz, Tap and African for the next 4 years at Bernice Johnson's Dance School in Jamaica Queens on full dance scholarship! He would also start taking acting classes as well. He would take the passion love and work ethic from football and now transfer it towards dance, entertainment, acting & producing.

NOW SERVING OTHERS: Lancelot would go on to create the "HIP-HOP DANCE BOOT CAMP TOUR" http://www.hip-hopdancebootcamp.com and AB-SOLUTE FUSION and recently developed a uniquely innovative core training program titled B2P2 Core Training: www.absolutefusionworkout.com

www.momzndahood.com/

One of Lancelot's proudest achievements has been to develop the concept of older mothers performing to professional hip-hop choreography. This concept has blossomed into "MOMZ-N-DA HOOD" phenom- moms

`HELPING THE HOMELESS: Lancelot is proud to be the youngest executive board member of the BETHANY HOUSE which is a homeless shelter based in Nassau Long Island NY for homeless woman and children. www.bhny.org

inspiration to us all!

LANCELOT THEOBALD <u>*Event Performer too*</u>! Overcoming injury & near death, he has risen to head **The Open End Repertory Theatre,** one of the best nationally! His dancing skills rival Fred Astaire's! Lancelot also has a film that was released in theatres in March of 2015. It's called **"At The Top Of The Pyramid".**

KRISTEN DOSCHER

Lancelot Theobald, Jr.

❖ ❖ ❖

The People of Distinction Humanitarian Awards is honored to present this Humanitarian Award to you for your wonderful contributions to our Human Family! We encourage you to continue your outstanding work enthusiastically into the future.

June 19, 2015

They Haven't Made An AX That Can Chop Down A Dream

They Haven't Made An AX That Can Chop Down A Dream

They Haven't Made An AX That Can Chop Down A Dream

They Haven't Made An AX That Can Chop Down A Dream

They Haven't Made An AX That Can Chop Down A Dream

Push-ups for charity
...an raised $10K for the Equal Justice Initiative

ALEXANDRA WHITBECK

Amid a global pandemic that fostered uncertainty and tests on all sides of the political spectrum, inspiration can be hard to find. But Lancelot Theobald Jr. used his passions for dance and fitness to facilitate change and created the Push Up Your Life campaign, a 10,000 push-up feat that raised $10,000 the Equal Justice Initiative.

Not only have Theobald's charitable actions benefited EJI, the Bethany House, as well, its efforts to tackle homelessness among women and children Long Island. Theobald sits on board of the Baldwin Bethany House.

Theobald said he grew characteristically depressed ate May, and attributed his sonality change partly to the death of George Floyd. On May Floyd, a 46-year-old Black man, died after a Minneapolis police officer, Derek Chauvin, pressed his knee into Floyd's neck for more than eight minutes before he stopped speaking moving.

"The whole George Floyd thing just completely affected me in a way that I never thought it would," Theobald said. "It sured a lot of things that, as a Black man, you learn to suppress, to keep going."

Theobald grew up in Brooklyn and moved to Long Island when he was 17. He recalled experiencing acts of discrimination and police brutality. The feelings flooded back as he watched similar events unfold.

"With the pandemic and everything, I started to get a little uncharacteristically depressed," he said. "I wasn't going to the gym — I couldn't go to the gym, actually, and I started getting things I haven't felt before."

Along with the inability to train and teach his clients or work on his numerous acting endeavors in person due to the COVID-19 pandemic, Theobald wasn't feeling like himself.

"Then I had a conversation with one of my dance groups, MZN-DA-HOOD, and for the first time, they were strangers about to I was going on," Theobald said. "And then I said actually, 'stuff has been going on for me.' This is a part of the fabric of DNA of America, quite frankly. But as we talked I started thinking, even though I needed to do something," MOMZ-N-DA-HOOD, he

explained, is a group of mothers that is known globally — the first in the world of break dancing mothers who learned how to dance in their forties and fifties. Theobald is the crew's director and choreographer.

Barbara Adler, founding member, dance captain and public relations director of MOMZ-N-DA-HOOD, has known Theobald for nearly two decades and recognized a change in her friend. Soon after, Adler and the other members of the dance crew held a Zoom meeting not to dance, but to talk.

"We also knew as a Black man in America he may be having a lot of feelings about what was going on," Adler said, "so we wanted to check in with him."

They devised a plan based on Theobald's tendency to push his fitness goals to the extreme. "He started talking about sometimes when he's really really like that he does these odd physical challenges and we kind of knew that about him," Adler said. "He'll do 5,000 sit-ups."

With a background in professional football transitioning to a career as a professional dancer and fitness trainer, Theobald was physically prepared for the challenge. His passion for fitness and dance is evident in his "ABSOLUTE FUSION" workout program and choreographing and directing MOMZ-N-DA-HOOD to national recognition. As Theobald said, "to have both of those disciplines together drove me to be able to accomplish 500 push-ups and stay consistent."

"The numbers are scary, but when you break it down and understand your discipline ... it becomes doable," he said. "But you have to be ready mentally and physically."

Push Up For Your Life began on July 1. Every time Theobald entered his home gym to do a set of 500 push-ups, he recorded the session, including rest periods to maintain the integrity of his project. He wanted donors and viewers to know he was accomplishing his goal and that their money was going to something real.

"It was very important to me that the people see everything," Theobald said. Whether it was streaming on Facebook Live or recordings sped up by Adler, the proof of every push-up can be found on the Push Up For Your Life Facebook page and @absolutefusionfitness on Instagram.

Adler used her marketing skills and charismatic personali-

ty to add another element to the Facebook live sessions, becoming the unofficial social media manager for Push Up For Your Life.

"It started getting a little boring with me just doing push-ups and sit-ups," Theobald said, which is where Adler's captivating personality came in.

The Facebook Live sessions of Theobald completing 500 push-ups went from one man exercising for a great cause to Adler bringing in children's instruments to entertain those who tuned in while chatting which each viewer.

"A little show developed," Adler said. "It got weird. I knew when people came on you have to engage with them, right? So I'm friendly and can be sometimes funny, so I would chit chat with the people coming on and that became like a show!"

The addition of the MOMZ-N-DA-HOOD captain received a great response from the audience and donations started to double, then triple.

The Push Up For Your Life campaign developed a community of supporters outside of those involved, and who directly related to Theobald. Some of the same viewers were making multiple donations, and the ferocity to reach 10,000 push-ups was tenfold.

"Unless you were going to kill me I was not going to stop," Theobald said. "It wasn't just about me anymore. It was about accomplishing this goal to help other people out. That's what motivated me to get up."

Adler noticed that the transformation for him was profound.

When the Push Up For Your Life Campaign neared its goal, Theobald began extensive research into which organization to donate the funds to, to make the biggest impact. He decided on the Equal Justice Initiative, a nonprofit organization dedicated to ending mass incarceration in the United States.

The check was mailed on Aug. 27 and the donation to EJI was received on Sept. 2, solidifying $10,632 going directly to a cause Theobald is "very affectionate about," due to directing "a whole documentary on a guy that was arrested and in jail for 40 years for something he didn't commit. Similar to EJI, a lawyer got his case and got him out after 40 years," Theobald said. This accomplishment is documented on the Push Up For Your Life Facebook page.

"I understand what it is to

Courtesy Push Up For Your Life/Facebook

LANCELOT THEOBALD JR. completed 10,000 push-ups to raise more than $10,000 for the Equal Justice Initiative as part of his Push Up For Your Life campaign.

have, but I also see what it is not to have," he said. "I always thought it was my responsibility to give back, use my talents in any way that I can to do something to give back."

"Everybody is the best that they can be when they're with Lance," Adler said.

To watch the mothers of MOMZ-N-DA-HOOD do what they do best, visit @momznda-hood on TikTok or momznda-hood.com for more information.

NEWS BRIEF
Share your thoughts on Baldwin's revitalization

Residents, consultants, and state and Town of Hempstead officials have taken the last few months to decide which potential developments will be submitted to the state as part of the effort to revitalize downtown Baldwin.

The process resumed — virtually — on Sept. 9 via Zoom after a months-long pause because of the coronavirus pandemic.

The latest meeting of the Local Planning Committee, comprising community leaders and business owners in Baldwin, took place on Sept. 16, where LPC members and consultants fielded questions from the public.

Baldwin received a $10 million grant from the state last year to overhaul the long-struggling downtown as part of the Baldwin Downtown Revitalization Initiative.

The group recently discussed three new transit-oriented and

mixed-use projects, which were proposed during the pause.

Most of the projects fall within the Baldwin zoning overlay district, which has a temporary zoning code to encourage developers to build there and revitalize the downtown, which has been blighted by vacant buildings for nearly 20 years.

The Town of Hempstead website shows an interactive virtual gallery room for residents to learn more about the Baldwin DRI. The virtual gallery room will remain open until Sept. 30 for participants to explore the proposed projects and share feedback through an online survey.

For more information about the Baldwin DRI, visit liherald.com/Baldwin for previous coverage and https://hempsteadny.gov/baldwin-dri on the Town of Hempstead website.

They Haven't Made An AX That Can Chop Down A Dream

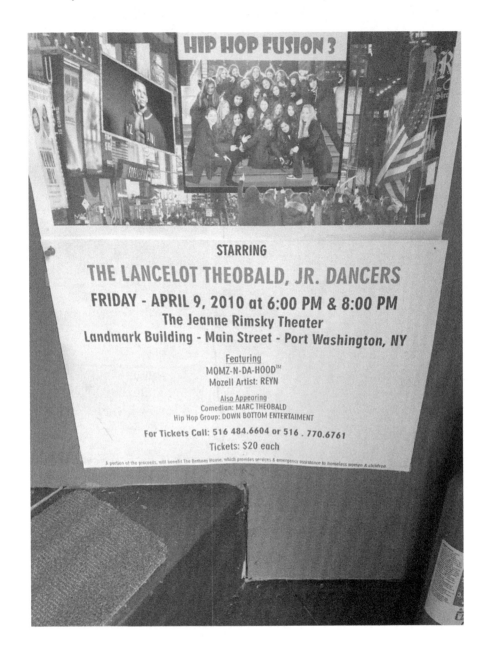

They Haven't Made An AX That Can Chop Down A Dream

They Haven't Made An AX That Can Chop Down A Dream

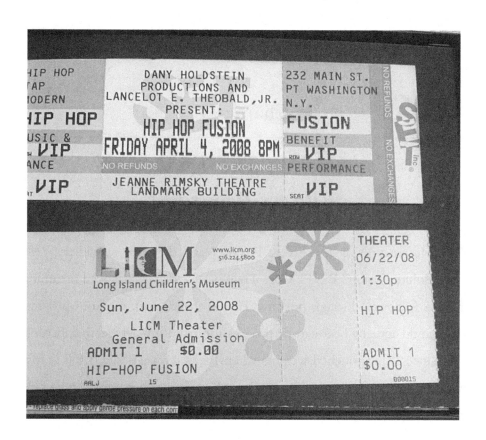

Chapter 9

Creation Of The Trademark Fitness Programs

The creation of "Ab-Solute Fusion," and then, the subsidiary, "Ab-Solute Fusion" B2/P2 Core Training. B2 means balanced breathing, and P2 is power through posture. This is a trademark workout program that would actually be a natural progression from my perspective, because ever since I first touched weights when I was ten years old, I fell in love with the concept of working out. One of my earlier heroes was my uncle, who stood at 6'1", 220 pounds, with 20-inch arms, sleek, just a handsome man—a great guy. He asked his sister, who is my mother, if he could store his weights at our house, because he had moved into another apartment that apartment wasn't big enough to house his weights.

She agreed for him to put his weight set in the basement. Anytime he would come over, I'd be so thrilled to see him. He was like one of those superhero uncles. Every time I saw him, I was just so excited. I would look at him and marvel. His body was incredible, and he was just such a good guy. When he left his weight set in the basement, I would go downstairs at ten years old and start playing with the weights. I wanted to look like him. Of course,

I didn't really know what I was doing, but I started lifting weights. I'd start bench-pressing the bar, pressing overhead, and curling. One thing led to another, and right around thirteen years old, I was playing for the Brooklyn Hurricanes, an incredible football organization in Marine Park, Brooklyn.

At thirteen, you had to make a weight limit each week, or you couldn't play. I was growing and had no real fat on me, but I would literally have to go down in the basement with a plastic bag, covering my entire upper body. They have plastic suits now, but I actually use to use plastic bags back in the day, and I would start working out with weights in order to lose weight. I'd sometimes have to lose 2 or 3 pounds within a week in order to be able to play on Sunday. That may seem like nothing, but when you have no fat on you, starting with 2 or 3 pounds every week is a task because if you're over one pound, you aren't allowed to play. It seemed absolutely insane for me not to be playing. So, I did everything in my power to lose this weight.

And I always would... Every week, I worked out downstairs with the weights. And then, on Sunday before the game, I'd be running around the park, losing that little bit of water so that I could make that weight requirement. That's how I got introduced to the weights. And then, by the time I got to high school, I noticed the majority of the kids hadn't been introduced to weights yet. By that time, I was well ahead of the game in terms of my strength, and my knowledge of how to lift. I started getting really serious in my junior year. And I started signing up for local gyms in Queens. I noticed right away that when I compared myself to others, I had these strong legs; naturally, everybody else I was around wasn't coming close to me. Then, I started focusing on nothing but my legs.

Now, if you know anything about working out, most people focus on the upper body and never really focus on their legs. I was focused on my legs and not really on my upper body, because this was the thing that was separating me from others. I began squatting. I mean, it became an obsession for me, just squatting and squatting, using more weight, I was doing leg extensions, lunges. I remember during my senior year in high school, there's a picture of me in the yearbook squatting over 450 lbs.

From that point on, as I attended college, I can honestly say that I have not missed more than seven consecutive days, in all the years that I've trained. My family and I all vacation together, and they know that whatever resort we go to has to have a workout facility, or else that's not the resort for us. It may sound a little obsessive, but a vacation for me goes something like this: We get up in the morning, we have breakfast, my wife goes to the pool, and I go to the gym. I work out for three to four hours. I meet her for lunch, and then we carry on our day with the family after that.

Some people read, and some people meditate; although I meditate also, this is the time for me to be with myself and work on myself. It's the one thing that I've maintained through all of the different transitions, and all these years when I've reinvented myself. The one constant is physical fitness. I have always come to this as my refuge, as a place for me to really dig down and be the best me that I can possibly be. I learned in college that you could try and take my scholarship away from me, and blackball me, but the one thing you can't take from me is my motivation to be the best me that I can be.

I've taken that discipline with me. Even when I danced, I still work out. You've got to figure, I was dancing in 14 to 20 classes a week, and I was going to the gym every day as well. This is something that I pride myself on. And so, of course, the natural occurrence of knowing myself and those five keys: knowing your worth, knowing that you're worthy, educating yourself, associating yourself around other people who have done it before, believing that you can achieve, and being able to put that work in. The natural progression for me was to create my own workout program. And that's what I did.

I started off teaching my first fitness class at Valencia Fitness which was a place where I've worked out at since I was seventeen. When I moved to Long Island from Brooklyn, I found the gym right near my house. It has been my alternate home since I was seventeen years old. The manager of the gym asked me to teach an abs class there, back in 2001.

I was known in the gym as being a lean, fit ex-athlete with an insane training regimen, and people liked me. So, I started teaching a class there in 2001. We scheduled the class in an area between the benches and the weights for about two years. Then, Valencia actually built a room in the gym, specifically for my class. About three years in, a guy by the name of Mike Macchia came into my class; he's been with me ever since. The reason I mentioned his name is because of the things I've done over the years. To be specific, the progressions, the constant building of skills, helping clients develop better strength, and creating different, unique exercises, has kept him coming on a regular basis for years. He shared how this class had changed his life. That was special and important to me. As a result, Mike and I became close over the years.

When he first stepped foot into the class, I could tell he was an athlete. And I said, "You got to be like a wrestler, or boxer, or something, because you just enjoy being abused." and he answered, "I was a wrestler." and I said, "I knew it!" The more exercises I came up with, that were core related, that hurt, his response seemed to just say 'Give me more'. He was energized by the reps and vigorousness. More and more people would look in, take the class, and then were dropping out of the class, because the class got so intense. I wanted to continue to tantalize, motivate, and 'up the ante' for Mike and some of the others. Everybody else had to hold on tight and go for the ride.

After a while, the three years turned into ten; I started creating different exercises for the core, as well as the entire body, including cardio. Using my philosophy that a person who believes must educate him/herself in whatever goal that you've set and surround yourself with people that are doing what you're doing. At that time, it seemed like the fitness craze Insanity was popular. Therefore, I started to embrace the insanity. I mean, at one point, we were doing like 1,000 jump rope, and 300 jumping jacks, in between all the other exercises. Soon, people were just falling off like flies. On the other hand, you had this core group of about six to seven girls and guys that stuck with it, and Mike was one of them. It just became this incredible class.

For years I worked to develop a more structured training regimen. Right around 2015, I decided to trademark a program called Ab-Solute Fusion Workout, Ab-Solute Fusion Fitness, which catered to athletes. I wanted to 'give back' in another meaningful way, besides monetarily. I felt it was important to find a way of giving every week. I mean, learning and creating new exercises, so that I could help these guys be at their physical best. And, by wholeheartedly participating, they were giving back to me. I was receiving, because as I was creating these new exercises, I was getting better and better as a teacher. Then, I started studying. I went back to school and earned my personal trainer's license. After that, I continued to further educate myself by studying to be a Performance Enhancement Specialist.

Ultimately, I was falling back on the keys, without even realizing it. Again, to reiterate, first of all, knowing your worth—knowing you're worthy of anything that your mind can conceive, you can achieve. I had dreamed about creating an exercise program, and I knew that I could do it, because the potential was established within me. I educated myself. I was constantly reading. I got a book that I keep with me to this day, that a friend of mine gave me. "The New Rules of Postures." It talks about the importance of posture, how to sit and stand, and the importance of the psoas muscle, which is deep in the body, very close to the spine. I had never really known about it; it's that inner core muscle that is so important for correct posture.

I got a book on plyometrics (The Shock Method) which was created by Yuri Verkhoshansky from East Germany in the late 1960s, early 1970s. I wanted to learn from the people who actually created it, or an extension of the people that created it. I also picked up a book called 'high-powered plyometrics: 77 advanced exercises for explosive sports training', written by James C. Radcliffe and Robert Farentinos. These are some things that I did to educate myself, to get better and better—to be the best that I can be.

After I trademarked the name Ab-Solute Fusion Workout & Ab-Solute Fusion Fitness, I catered it to athletes. Then, I reached out to my contacts, acquaintances, as well as other people I knew. Relying on my good graces as a person, I returned to my high school coach to see if I could develop a program with the football team. He said, absolutely. I implemented the program for four years. It was an incredible workout. He said it was the best work out program the school had ever had at Holy Cross in his forty years.

I asked him to endorse me on video; he obliged. The program I created wound up getting shared with another coach I grew up with from the old neighborhood in Brooklyn. He felt it was also good for his basketball athletes.

This athletic program enhances core strength, helps develop explosive power, strength, balance, and agility. In creating this program, I used my dance and football background combined with knowledge I gained from reading and studying about the human body. In the process, although people don't really talk about it, is that dancers are superb athletes.

I'll never forget the first time someone mentioned that. My response was, "You're out of your mind!" Then, after becoming a dance student, and experiencing what the depth of their training can be, I had to agree. I soon found out that many times they are better athletes than football and basketball players. Both sets are basically trying to achieve certain levels in their field, but the approach is completely different.

Dancers need balance, core strength, good posture and technique. At times they also need explosive power and definitely, agility. What do Athletes in other sports need? The same thing. They may train differently, but all genres of sports need strength and a skill set to be at the top of their 'game'. My dance training and knowledge, along with the studies, information, and training I have as an athlete, allowed me to come up with a program that can benefit anyone. That's how B2/P2 Core Training evolved. It is a multi-dimensional, whole body fitness program. Its emphasis is developing inner core strength and balance.

There are over a hundred innovative exercises that utilize foam rollers, combined with the use of basic kettlebell exercises. It's a different kind of powerful, fun training experience. Now, I have at my disposal for teaching athletes two workout programs. After working with the coach from Holy Cross High School, I hooked up with head coach Dwayne Mitchell of Scanlan High School, and the director of one of the most popular basketball organizations in New York City, the Gauchos. For a few years I would work with their athletes, their training began at 6 a.m on Saturdays. Then, Dwayne and I began traveling to Grenada and Trinidad. We also flew to

Canada to teach basketball skills and drills. The B2-P2 Training program helped transform players into dynamic, formidable athletes who later earned scholarships and were recruited by various colleges. In testimony to this fact, when asked,

Tom Pugh, head coach of Holy Cross Knights football for over forty years said,

"I would definitely not tell our competitors because I see the results, but not every program can handle Ab-Solute-Fusion. You have to... It's a commitment and... Because if you just come in and do it once or twice a year, it's not going to work. The kids have to be prepared for this. This is not easy."

Lancelot Theobald Jr.:

Now, do you see this being something that can transcend into basketball and other athletics?

Coach Pugh:

Absolutely because we already see that. The kid that goes far in sports today, whether he's a quarterback, or a forward on the basketball team, never mind what sport they play... They all get these personal trainers. Everybody knows personal trainers are a big business today. One-on-one training to teach kids how to play. I'm old school. So, I'm not all into the whole personal training thing, but you know what? We're getting it for a group session, so that's why it's so valuable.

Lancelot Theobald Jr.:

Coach, you've been coaching for over 42 years, and you've seen a lot of different workout programs, and you've done a lot of conditioning. Do you feel the Ab-Solute-Fusion workout program is preparing these kids for that next level?

Coach Pugh:

Absolutely. First of all, the Ab-Solute-Fusion program doesn't... It's not going to work in every program. You'd have to have kids who want to go to the next level. You need kids who are highly motivated athletically to make it through this program, and like I said, it's like having a personal trainer, and these kids want to get to the next level. We have a lot of kids playing college football. 39 this year, 42 last year. We have... many of the kids go on to play, and you're not going to get there if you don't have a tremendous work ethic, and this program ensures that. The Ab-Solute-Fusion program ensures that.

In another interview:

Lancelot Theobald Jr.:

I'm sitting here with Dwayne Mitchell, director for the Gauchos located in the Bronx NY, and first of all, Dwayne, I want to say thank you for allowing Ab-Solute-Fusion Fitness workout to be a part of the Gauchos for the last month.

Lancelot Theobald Jr.:

I'm just wondering what your assessment is on the program and the concept of working the core and developing conditioning, agility, explosiveness, quickness, and flexibility through these different exercises.

Dwayne Mitchell:

Well, it's a blessing for you to be here and to introduce the Absolute Fusion Workout to the athletes, because I've been doing basketball for a long time, and I'm fortunate to have your program... be a part of our program as we help develop a more complete athlete which we haven't had and so to have that in our program and to be able to give the athletes and the kids here that particular ingredient and what it takes to become a complete athlete, it's great because they've got to have a strong core which is going to make them more explosive and make them more athletic. So, it's great.

Lancelot Theobald Jr.:

And you definitely see where it works with basketball players, football players, soccer, and athletes in general; all can utilize this type of program.

Dwayne Mitchell:

It's a universal program; baseball, basketball, all athletes got to have that certain just athleticism that allows them to be who they are in reference to being explosive, being athletic... Just being at a certain level, and then the Ab-Solute-Fusion Workout gives those athletes that particular ingredient, once again, that help take them to another level.

Lancelot Theobald Jr.:

So, what do you know about taking things to another level? You're a coach now. Tell me a little background on yourself.

Dwayne Mitchell:

Well, I've been coaching for a long time; I've been coaching for over forty years, and I've just been blessed to be able to still be able to coach the game of basketball. So right now, it's just like an obligation on my part to be able to reach out to people like yourself that have a program that benefits athletes. So, like I said, to meet this level of longevity in this sport this is something that's needed for me to make my athletes better. I thank you for taking the time to come in at six in the morning, and you show a commitment and dedication to better the athletes. The parents love it. I mean, that's why they're here. They ask for you, like are you going to be here today? You know, they look forward to your presence.

:

In other testimonials for B2/P2 Core Training,

Stefanie Balistreri says, "Being a mom of two toddlers leaves me little time, but the B2/P2 Core Training has put me in the best shape of my life while getting a bonus massage at the same time."

Mike Macchia says, "The B2/P2 Core Training hits muscles I didn't know existed. I walk better and even feel taller because of the power I feel. It's all about balance, posture, and breathing. My upper body and legs get a workout. Also, the strength I feel is immeasurable."

:

Laura Chabla says, "Very few workouts deliver what they promise, but my body has changed since I started doing the B2/P2 Core Training. I can honestly say I apply my new form and breathing technique to not just my other workouts but to other physical activities, I do. Nothing is more exciting than seeing progress and nothing is more addicting than the B2/P2 Core Training experience."

:

In retrospect I think I developed a competitive instinct, a drive, a fierce work ethic because, from the time I was a young kid, I was always on a winning programs and always had to compete with other exceptional athletes just to get a spot on the team. Back then, when I was playing little league, we had 60 and 70 kids that would try out for the team. I played for the Hurricanes in Brooklyn, and Brooklyn Hurricanes were known just as a winning program.

And then, I went to Holy Cross High School, which was another winning program, and I remember my coach recruited me from the Hurricanes to be a part of another winning program. And I think I developed, between that and having to wake up five o'clock every morning and travel from Brooklyn and take two trains and a bus to Queens just to go to school. It instilled in me what it meant to love something so much that you would give anything or be willing to give up everything to be a part of it because it's difficult to get up at five o'clock every morning, have your father drive you to the train station, take two trains and a bus just to get to school and play football but what that taught me was that tenacity, it taught me sacrifice. It taught me dedication, and I mean, I didn't know it at the time, but it would set me up. It gave me the foundation to be the person I am today.

They Haven't Made An AX That Can Chop Down A Dream

They Haven't Made An AX That Can Chop Down A Dream

Welcome to AB-SOLUTE-FUSION® WORKOUT

They Haven't Made An AX That Can Chop Down A Dream

They Haven't Made An AX That Can Chop Down A Dream

They Haven't Made An AX That Can Chop Down A Dream

They Haven't Made An AX That Can Chop Down A Dream

They Haven't Made An AX That Can Chop Down A Dream

They Haven't Made An AX That Can Chop Down A Dream

They Haven't Made An AX That Can Chop Down A Dream

They Haven't Made An AX That Can Chop Down A Dream

They Haven't Made An AX That Can Chop Down A Dream

They Haven't Made An AX That Can Chop Down A Dream

They Haven't Made An AX That Can Chop Down A Dream

Chapter 10

Love-Hate Relationship, That Is Teaching

I wasn't going to write a chapter on teaching. I have a real love-hate relationship with being a teacher. However, I happened to talk to a friend of mine who said, "Come on, that's a big part of who you are, and you can't ignore that." One of the reasons why I have an issue with teaching is because I never planned on going to college with the idea of ever being an educator. Missing out on dancing school as a youngster, meant that I didn't get that invaluable experience of going through the ranks, as I grew older. I attended dance school as an adult. In my head, I had put myself through a four-year intensive program with the sole purpose of becoming a dancer, not a teacher.

It just so happened that another friend, Melanie Perkins, had opened up a dance studio right at the height of the period when I was 'Sir Lancelot', dancing, auditioning and getting work. I had just worked at the Metropolitan Opera House for the last three seasons. I wasn't thinking about instructing at all. She asked me, "Look, I'm opening up a school in Westbury, and I'd love for you to come down and teach tap."

I reluctantly said yes to this new opportunity because I knew I'd have to head to a studio after getting home at four, or five o'clock in the morning. It meant getting up at eight to be ready for class at nine. I would be exhausted, and to top it off, I was assigned to teach little kids.

Ironically, I actually met my wife during this period of time. We have been married for fifteen years now, but I met her teaching her daughter at Melanie's dance school. Melanie and Patrice became good friends. Melanie said, "How would you like to go out with Lancelot, the tap teacher?" she said, "Sure," and the rest is history.

I was teaching Patrice's daughter tap lessons, as she had signed up for one of the classes. Cidney was six years old at the time, and she was a great helper. She use to always help me with the other kids. But, from my perspective, it was like babysitting. You'd be trying to teach the kids, and then they'd sit down, "I don't want to tap." I wasn't use to that. I had no idea how to handle that, and I was exhausted. At one point, I distinctly remember the kids complaining and saying, "I don't want to tap. I'm tired." I said, "Is everybody tired?" they bellowed, "Yes!" I said, "Okay, this is what we're going to do. Everybody hold hands, lie down, close your eyes, and dream about doing shuffles. We're going to have sleep time." The kids were like, "Yaaay, sleep time!" And literally, we went to sleep holding hands in a circle. I was actually passed out sleeping, for real! They didn't want to be there, and I was tired, so it made total sense to me.

All the classes took place in one gym; you had the adults taking class in one area, and you had other groups of kids taking a class in another area of the space, and then you had us in one corner. After a couple of weeks of "Sleep time," Melanie came to me; she said, "You can't keep sleeping like that with the kids. The parents are looking." I said, "Well, the kids wanted to sleep. So, I figured we'd do a whole sleep game." she said, "No, no, no, you can't do that." I didn't know, and even if I did know, I was so exhausted. I said, "If they don't want to dance, heck, I don't want to teach" but I wound up teaching vs sleeping.

Melanie was a sweetheart and a good friend. She was the first person to plant the seed that I could possibly reinvent myself once again and be an educator. It was something that I never expected, never wanted to do, but she now was putting this in front of me as an option.

When Melanie's school closed, she happened to meet a lady who had another studio in an upscale area on Long Island. She asked me if I was interested in going with her. Melanie, I guess, saw the potential in me as a teacher and looked past the sleeping incidents. I was reluctant at first, because now, I wasn't just teaching for a friend; I was really putting myself out there as a teacher. This experience caused a major shift in my mental state. It was a beautiful school in a great area, and the executive director was a wonderful lady who, like Melanie, saw something in me as a teacher and gave me an opportunity to teach several classes at her school. I pay homage to her all the time because she gave me a shot. This lady didn't know me from a can of paint and gave me the opportunity to teach a class at her school in this upscale area.

I started with one class, which was very successful. It was an adult class of tap dancers, who hadn't been taking class for many years, they just happened to find this class because they wanted to get back into tap. Those were the people that I was thrilled to deal with. They knew how to take class, they appreciated it, and they were the first ones to tell me, "We love your class. We love your technique. I've been taking tap class for many years, and the way you explain it, and break it down is different. We love it." I was like, 'wow, I can get used to this teaching thing!' I think one of the reasons why was because I had learned tap as an adult. I remembered how I just adored my teachers; and now, there were adult students seeing me the same way I saw and felt about my teachers—I loved it.

When I was studying tap, I started focusing on the shifting of the body weight, and watching what the body was specifically doing during the transition of the different tap steps. I started to hone in on what the legs and hips were doing, and not just how the feet were executing the step. I noticed that the hips and your core gave you better control over how the sound was being executed. Suddenly, I started coming up with a technique without really even knowing it. Plus, I started picking up the steps faster. Soon, I was able to articulate them faster and faster.

Additionally, I was able to apply that information to the adults that were struggling through some of the same things I went through, in terms of trying to understand 'how to' do certain steps. More importantly, I needed to show them how to control their sounds. Fortunately, I was able to give them that information that no one else had given them before. And they loved the class.

Younger students started enrolling in the class; and ultimately, that didn't work. The younger students weren't as seasoned at taking a class like the older students. They were talkative and disruptive in class. The adults, after a while, petered off, and they stopped coming.

By that time, I started getting more classes, and I began teaching hip hop. Hip hop was becoming very popular at that time. It was new for this area, and 'the' thing to do. I had several classes, and I was making money.

Unfortunately for me, there were some kids in these classes who really didn't come to learn how to dance; they came to socialize and have fun with their friends. There is nothing wrong with taking a class and having fun. The problem was, I truly didn't understand that concept. Dance had changed my life, gave me life, and I didn't understand the notion of just having 'fun'. I was taking a class to be a dancer. It was very serious for me. There were kids in classes of nine to ten students, and maybe six or seven of them were friends. They came, basically, to socialize with their friends for an hour. The parents dropped them off to have an hour to do whatever they wanted. Here I was, trying to really teach. I had already committed to trying to be the best teacher I could possibly be.

I've learned over the years that a majority of kids who I have taught, take dance and do sports as recreation. It's something to do to broaden their horizons or add to their resume. The more extracurricular activities you do, the more appealing you are to colleges down the line. I had no idea; so, we clashed—we clashed big time. In my mind, I was like, "Listen, you're not disrespecting me!" The way I saw it, these students were not listening and being rude by talking while I was talking. It felt like they were completely ignoring what I was saying. So, I started having the kids sit down; and, every week, I had to reprimand them. Soon, the parents started complaining. In my mind, I'm telling myself, "I'm just trying to teach. Your kid is disrespectful. She or he is not listening." Eventually, I came to terms with the fact that I saw everything through a narrow lens based on what I thought teaching was supposed to be. It was my lack of knowledge and understanding that caused me to be reactive to this situation.

What did the parents do? They took their kid and the six or seven friends out of the class. I was shocked! I said to myself, "Wow! That's how it works around here."

I had to realize that the kids were taking classes in packs of five, or six friends. They'd have you start a whole new class with all of their friends, and the moment you reprimand them, or if they didn't like how the class was going, they'd take all the kids out, and move to another class. Sometimes they'd move to another studio! Then, to top it off, you would see these same kids in town, and they'd walk past you without even speaking. What?? I was like, "Ohhhh no, they didn't! Oh, okay. That's how it works around here!" In retrospect, I should have handled it differently; but remember, I didn't go to school for teaching, or behavior management. I handled it the best way I knew how at the time, my response was just as immature—I started doing the exact same thing. I'd see students in town and wouldn't speak to them. Of course, I learned that wasn't the right way to handle the adversity; it was all new to me. I wasn't handling this transition into teaching very well. I adored my teachers, respected my teachers, and now I'd experienced quite a rude awakening.

I missed two important keys. 1. Educating yourself on what it is that you're doing and 2. Surrounding yourself with people who have successfully done it before.

In retrospect, the two missing keys would have helped me to understand that many kids take dance classes and play sports for recreation, and there is nothing wrong with that. In fact, it's healthy to participate in different activities. It makes you well-rounded.

For me, if I got involved with something, I was trying to be the best at it; therefore, I approached it with a certain mindset. It wasn't the student who needed to change; I needed to change. As a teacher, you have to be able to recognize the different types of students and adjust accordingly. I've learned to be proactive, instead of reactive.

I loved making money but had a love-hate relationship with teaching at that point. I had a problem adjusting to the different types of students. Every week, I regretted teaching certain classes; because in my mind, I had created what the teaching experience should be. I know how I admired and respected my former teachers. Thank God I started teaching private tap and hip hop lessons. 1:1 classes were like my savior, because the kids taking private lessons really wanted to learn. And that's when I started to like teaching. I had one student who used to come to the studio with his sister when he was three years old. He'd watch me teach a private tap student while his sister was taking ballet class. At three years old, he was enamored by the tap sounds and rhythms; and by the time he was five, or six, his mom had to sign him up with me. She exclaimed 'That's all he talked about.' I worked with him until he was a teenager.

Melanie also wound up running a dance program at a community center on high street in Manhasset, NY, funded by the Great Neck Arts Center. Melanie initially ran the program, and she brought me over to teach the tap. This was where I got my first opportunity to choreograph routines for younger dancers to perform at different venues. I loved it. These kids were super talented and eager to learn and perform. After about two years, Melanie left the program to relocate, and I then headed up this dance program. We performed at Great Adventure, Hershey Park, Madison Square Garden, and Radio City Music Hall. As a result of our performance at Madison Square Garden and Radio City Music Hall, I was offered a job as the Knick City Dancers' choreographer. Soon after that, I choreographed an episode for the hit MTV series," Skins".

And then, I moved to another studio in Roselyn, NY, called the JCC, where I created "Momz-N-Da Hood," known around the world as America's first professionally choreographed group of break dancing/hip hop dancing mothers in their 50 & 60s. The original members were: Barbara, Sue, Audrey, Susan & Barry. All the dancer/moms past and present of MNDH are my pride & joy. We are a part of Hip Hop history, as we were the first commercial group to bridging the gap between young and old in regards to hip hop dance. We showed the world that "Anything Is Possible At Any Age." I went on to Patti Krieners's studio in Glen Cove, where I worked with Nikki Blonsky, who wound up being one of the stars of the iconic movie, "Hair Spray" with John Travolta. While teaching at High Street one of the student's mother who was also a dance instructor invited me to teach at a studio, she taught at called Berest Dance Center in Port Washington, NY. Her name was Karen Ferby-Guy. She said she noticed my ability as a young male teacher, to motivate and encourage the kids to attack and articulate quality hip hop movement. She believed I would be an asset to their studio. At Berest I was blessed to be surrounded by ex-professional dancers and dance teachers, and I began to learn the art of being a dance instructor. Then, I began to teach at "Two Worlds" in Greenvale, NY, where I produced/directed/choreographed/danced in a sold-out show called "Hip Hop Fusion", for four years, worked with pop artists Madison Beer, Daniel Drazin, and Heather Burns from the Tony Award-Winning Broadway show "Billy Elliot." I worked with and trained Justin Hall from "Mary Poppins" and I teach hip hop & tap at that studio. It all started because Melanie introduced me to Regina Gil, who gave me the opportunity to teach the High Street EOC program, funded by the Great Neck Art Center. They saw something in me that I hadn't seen in myself. I went from having a love-hate relationship with teaching to learning how to utilize a natural ability I had to: teach, motivate, create, develop, influence, and shape ideas that would impact American pop culture.

Ironically, a great deal of my creativity that was being utilized during this incredible time was coming from an adult class of women who were lawyers, a doctor, a nurse, business owners, and a ex-dancer who all were full time mothers. You had: Monelle, Dr. Deb, Karen, Arlene RN, Ester Esq, Jessica, Debi Esq. This was my adult hip-hop class at Two Worlds. We've been together for over fifteen years, and they're the ones that really, really brought the best out of me. I was giving to them, but I was on the receiving end, because they were giving me their best. This allowed me to give my best and create. To date, we have over fifteen years of choreography, and nothing has been duplicated. We do three weeks with one song, and then we move on. Do you know how many routines and how much creativity that is? This class was my lab, similar to a rapper's pen and pad; I would come up with movement in my head many times while in class, and by the end of the hour, they were able to show me what it looked like. I became efficient in the female-style hip-hop movement. I could see and create it, but I needed that fluid movement of a girl's hips and torso to really visualize the movement. They were able to actualize the movements.

This is why I was able to choreograph film, video, and TV. My mind was constantly being massaged, and these ladies were kneading it. As much as I was giving to them, they were giving to me. Additionally, I had the teenage students from Two Worlds. Initially, a majority of them weren't extremely talented, but what they did have was commitment and drive. They personified dedication, desire, and discipline to be the best that they could possibly be. By the time I got finished with them, those kids were going to college and passing dance team auditions in their first year. In them, I instilled my mantra that, "I don't need the best dancer; I need the hardest worker because I can make the hardest worker into the best dancer."

We have a professional dancer that's out there now doing her thing in California. Like I mentioned earlier, we had one girl that left to do Billy Elliot on Broadway and received a "Tony" with the rest of the cast, then came back to me, after her tenure in "Billy Elliot" for two years, and did Hip Hop Fusion 4, "The Journey."

These are the experiences that turned my love-hate relationship with teaching into a viable option. I found a way to make teaching work for me, working towards my ultimate goal of continuing to better myself, and grow as an artist.

One of the many things I learned during this journey is that nothing lasts forever. You must stay focused on whatever your long-term goals are. Sometimes, you must change course when things don't feel right, or are negatively affecting your vision. Once those four years of Hip Hop Fusion had concluded, I noticed that the next phase of students who were coming up didn't have the same passion and fire. They wanted to do the show but were not willing to put that work in—taking classes twice a week, consistently. I could feel the shift; I could see the writing on the wall. I knew these kids. If they weren't willing to sacrifice time to put in the maximal effort, there was no way we were going to have the success we had previously. Ultimately, I decided to end the production after four years. It was a tough decision, but one that had to be made.

One of the many good things that came out of my time with Hip Hop Fusion was that it exposed the community to hip hop dance. Suddenly, I went from teaching a few classes of teenagers and adults, to teaching multiple classes of hip hop for kids of all ages. I was making money, but it was again at the cost of my sanity. My classes were packed, but they weren't enjoyable. In fact, it became torturous. I started feeling that love-hate relationship with teaching again; and then, it became a problem for me. My journey through life taught me that making money at the cost of your sanity and happiness affects you as an artist, and keeping your eye on your long-term objective is the key to success. So, I made up my mind that it was best for me not to teach certain age groups. I learned that male teachers teaching little girls, hyped up on sugar, can sometimes be tricky, even problematic. As a result, my classes dwindled in the next few years, but I was okay with that. I couldn't have been happier. I had fewer classes, but in the classes I did have, the kids were learning; I was teaching and creating, which was keeping me in line with my overall objective. My focus was to continue to grow as an artist. I was able to generate income in several different ways. I've always had many 'irons in the fire', so to speak, because one thing I've learned as an artist, is you never rely on one source of income. If that 'one' thing goes, then your rent, car note, and groceries go with it. Teaching class was just one thing I did to generate income. I never turned down income unless I had other options to fall back on. I was able to say, "No, I'm not doing this. No, I'm not doing that," because I knew I had several things to fall back on. I didn't reject offers to be mean or arrogant; I did it because I believed in those five keys and my overall objective. Over the years, I have stayed true to my goal which is to continue to grow as a person and artist; so that when an opportunity presents itself, I am ready.

Interestingly enough, in March 2020, a world pandemic occurred, called covid which would impact everything, everywhere. The country (and the world) was forced to shut down. Uncertainty loomed on every level—personally, socially, economically, mentally, physically… for the first time, I was experiencing the feelings of depression and anxiety. Many months into the pandemic, we started teaching classes on zoom. Early on, I realized that the kids who were 'zooming' to class during covid really, really wanted to be there. I also understood that as educators, we had a responsibility to bring joy to these students in the midst of uncertainty, fear, and in some instances, depression. I was truly empathetic because I was experiencing some of the same feelings. What I did, instead of teaching my curriculum, I found out what they were watching and listening to, and then incorporated that into what I was teaching. For the first time, my approach was all about bringing joy and happiness to my students first. I watched TikTok, found out the different dances that were popular, and incorporated some of those movements into what I was teaching. It was about compromising and changing for the good of the students, while still staying true to my overall objective. The two can coexist, and I'm forever grateful for this realization at a time when a change needed to be made.

For me, teaching has become about how I can positively affect my students through the arts and stay connected to my overall objective of continuing to grow as an artist. I now had my finger on the pulse of what was influencing this next generation of movement. I was learning from my students. It was this give-and-take that was working. I realized that the joy of dance sometimes comes from just being in the room with friends, doing, and being a part of the influences of pop culture.

. Ironically, the silver lining in all of this was I learned how to be more flexible and open to learning from them, which broadened my creative pallet. I learned psychologically, when students feel validated and appreciated for what they know and have to offer, they are more invested in learning and class participation. It showed me a new way to approach teaching. Thanks to covid, I see things differently now.

When I played sports, I always played sports to be the best l could be. I learned how to dance to be the best dancer I could possibly be. As an exotic dancer, I danced to be the best I could be. I didn't discern that you may participate in activities/sports, just to be having recreational fun. As the saying goes, 'I just wasn't built like that.' And that's what I met up with, many students that were there for recreation, to have fun. My journey exposed me to students with extraordinary potential, yet they may see dance as just a hobby. They're not trying to do it as a profession. That was completely foreign to me, but these experiences were educating me, and would prove to be super beneficial and helpful down the line. As a teacher, I was now utilizing those five keys again. I knew my worth and knew I was worthy of being a teacher. I continued to educate myself by being open to learning, and at times, shifting my mindset. I associate myself with other teachers—successful teachers. I was willing to put the work in. Most importantly, I believed I could achieve.

As a result, when I was hired to choreograph for the feature film "At the Top of the Pyramid," which was in theaters, I choreographed 11 scenes. That was a humongous responsibility for a first-time film choreographer who was working with actors; and 95% of them were not dancers. Ironically, I was prepared for that because I had dealt with this dilemma over the last ten years with kids who started off with minimal ability but had a good work ethic. They listened and was able to transform themselves into hip-hop dancers.

It was a monumental task, but I was able to get these actors looking like hip-hop dancers, ready to be showcased in a movie. One of the things I did was approach the producers and said, "Listen, the schedule that you have currently is not going to work." based on the schedule they gave, I knew we would not have these actors ready and looking sharp for the shoot. So, I made an appeal, "Listen, you're going to have to put some more rehearsal time in here."

I had no clue that more rehearsal time would cost thousands of dollars more, because this was a union gig. I said, "Listen, you do whatever you got to do. We need many more hours of rehearsals because these actors are not ready..." luckily, they went to the executive producers and cleared me for more rehearsal time. As a result, those actors were 'on point' when it was time to say "Action!"

I was able to get to that point with "At the Top of the Pyramid," based on the wealth of education and knowledge I obtained from the past ten years of working with, and teaching students at Two Worlds and Berest. It was actually a good thing, because I knew exactly how to handle these actors who were not dancers, in order to transform them into dancers, in a short period of time. I also knew what it was like to deal with talented kids who picked up quicker and articulated my movement differently. I had worked with dancers at High Street.

If I had only worked with kids, like the kids from High Street, I don't think I'd have been able to do "At the Top of the Pyramid". Those kids were super talented, they picked up choreography quickly; and, I didn't have to break down the movements to them. They understood the basic foundations of hip hop; they were a part of hip hop culture. Whereas, when I dealt with Hip Hop Fusion kids, I had to teach them from the ground up. I had to help them understand how to bend their knees, how to pop their back, and how to give me that energy I needed. The kids were willing and eager to suck up this information, and they started looking good.

I was able to teach these actors on the movie set what to do, because I was able to recognize what they needed. Actors were attempting to do the moves, and they weren't bending their knees. Hip hop is a form of African dance— it is all about the ground; it's in the ground. I had to first teach them the fundamentals of bending and leaning. You've got to 'sit' that butt back. Your power's in the back part of your legs, and your butt. Push through the floor and pop up. You can make any movements more dynamic by using the energy from the floor and leaning.

All the things that I was able to bring to the movie set were a direct result of all the things that I had learned and experienced as a teacher. I had taken the love-hate relationship with teaching, and made it work. When life gives you lemons, you make lemonade; and trust me, somewhere down the line in this incredible journey called life, making lemonade will come in handy; it will become your asset.

They Haven't Made An AX That Can Chop Down A Dream

They Haven't Made An AX That Can Chop Down A Dream

Conclusion

THe invaluable five keys to reinvention set me on this incredible journey through life that has been filled with adventure, love, friendship, compassion, growth, disappointment, excitement and possibilities. It has kept me hungry, young, vibrant, and unafraid to still dream of being and doing anything I put my mind to. The greatest gift to me, though, is the gift of happiness. These five keys to reinvention unlocked the doors to my inner joy, which is priceless to me. The ability to share my happiness with others and teach the five keys to reinvention is what I truly think God wants me to do. I took those five keys and instilled them into a group of older ladies twenty, years ago, who started dancing with me for exercise. I recognized in them some of the same traits I identified in myself as they were trying something new and experiencing something different. They were taking a hip-hop class with me at a time when it was considered a dance form for young urban kids, not middle age white women. They were comfortable in their own skin and didn't seem to care about what their peers thought. They struggled, had this tenacity and endearing quality about them. They were getting together on weekends, just to be prepared for class the next week. I began to educate and teach them the different styles of hip-hop dance, as well as where it originated from. I surrounded them with younger hip-hop dancers. They were exposed to some of the legends in the hip-hop community. They invested twenty-one years of blood, sweat, and commitment to this dance form. Most importantly, I got them to buy into and believe, first and foremost, that they should be taken seriously. As a result, they are now known across the globe as the world's first professionally choreographed group of hip hop/break dancing mothers floating in their 50s & 60s. Their trademarked name is Momz-N-Da Hood. You've seen them on television commercials, videos, the news, a game show, talk shows, newspapers, magazines, etc. If these five keys to reinvention can work for Momz-N-Da Hood, it stands to reason these five keys can work for anyone.

I thank you for taking the time to travel through my journey of life. I hope you've learned from my experiences that "Anything is possible at any age" when you follow those five keys. What I've learned in writing this book is that my journey is just beginning. I have a whole lot more life to live with endless possibilities in front of me. When you can take your negatives, turn them into your positives. Acknowledge the things that hurt you the most and use them as fuel to ignite the full potential that is locked inside of you. When you tap into your full potential, you will find the diverse possibilities inside of you that will open your mind to happiness and ultimate success.

About the author

Lancelot Theobald, Jr. Is a man who does it all: sports, acting, dancing, choreography, producing, philanthropy work, keynote speaking, entrepreneurship, fitness guru, teacher, executive board member, author, etc. His early success as an athlete gave him a taste of what it was like to compete for a position, to work hard and be a part of a team.

Lancelot attended Holy Cross High School. Upon graduating with a full scholarship in hand, success followed him to the University of Maine, after he had gone through what he coined as the "Tragic four episodes." Withstanding those experiences would propel him to college, where he clashed head on with adversity, stood face to face with success and went from a boy to a man. After graduating with a degree in communications, Lancelot went on to play football in Europe. His willingness to pursue any and everything to achieve his dream, is the only way he knows how to approach life.

Lancelot made the incredible transition from athletics to dance, by attending dance school as an adult, studying, and becoming a professional dancer. He is considered one the first athletes to ever successfully make that transition as an adult. He then combined the two disciplines, athletics and dance, to develop a trademark workout program, "Ab-Solute Fusion,"

B2/P2 Core Training. This unique program is utilized by athletes from all different sports, and of all ages.

Lancelot's most recent credits includes Amazon Prime's movie "Hilo 3," producer/actor in the play "Relationships," actor, choreographer/dancer in a movie currently streaming on several platforms around the world: "Eddie." He's appeared on TBS's hit series with Tracy Morgan, the "Last OG," author, as well as, serving as professional coach and mentor. Lancelot's combination of internal optimism and his unique ability to always be comfortable in his own skin has always allowed him to think 'outside the box.' He never limits the goals he wants to accomplish. It didn't matter that it hadn't been done before. His faith compelled him to do it. He lives by a code that he instills in others that surround him: "It doesn't matter if it hasn't been done before, be the first, because anything is possible, at any age. All you have to do is truly believe."

Lancelot is most proud of his work with the Bethany House, a homeless shelter for women and women with children, in Nassau County, NY. He came to Bethany House many years ago, seeking an organization that 'Hip Hop Fusion,' his production company could support. Lancelot has been involved with Bethany House ever since. Lancelot has also served on Bethany's Board of Directors, since 2009. Presently, he is the Vice Chair for the Program & Development Committee. Lancelot is also proud of the fact Bethany House, as an organization, is changing the face of how homelessness is being dealt with. They are showing the world that it's not enough to just provide housing for the homeless. You must also provide resources to help fix what is broken. So often, if you lose your home, your foundation is rocked and shaken emotionally, spiritually, and psychologically. Bethany House is providing different programs aimed at helping you first and foremost heal from the inside out and then providing the guests with the proper tools to help them never set foot back in a shelter system again.

Testimonials

THe end of the school year. Everyone is back or heading home for the summer. I decided to make a trip to New York with a girlfriend at the time, Veronica, and my nephew, Eric. He needs to make a pickup/drop off, and I had a small window of time to make it happen before I had to start a summer gig and chill.

So, I reached out to my sister to let her know we were planning to come up. I asked if we could stay overnight, along with Veronica. I stopped in Brooklyn first, to drop off a few things.

As we headed out to Long Island via the Belt Parkway, we reached my sister's house, whose Lance's mother. It was always very nice to see big sister. The house phone rang. Lil Lance called the house and told us to come over to Queens; he was hanging with Cousin Paul, Jimmy (Lance's old neighborhood friend from Brooklyn), and one of Paul's homeboys from the Queens neighborhood.

We get there, and it was always great seeing Lance. I was also glad to see Paul. He's really special, he and I hadn't seen each other in quite a while. Lance sees Cousin Eric and introduced himself to Veronica. As we were hanging/catching up, they started talking about going down to the beach. It wasn't too late, or so we thought. So, I thought it was a good idea, especially since it was Veronica's first time hanging out in NYC. We wanted to show her as many sites as possible while we were here.

It was late in the day, so we were able to get parking spots close to the entrance. We headed down to the beach to find a spot to chill. We found a spot to set up the blanket; Veronica had no plans to go into the water but didn't mind chilling. Eric also stayed on the beach, which in hindsight, turned out to be the best move.

I joined Lance, Paul, and the rest of the guys as we proceeded into the water. At first, things were just fine; the water was a little cool, but comfortable. It was late in the day, at the time, so I didn't put it together. The tide was coming in, and the water was becoming more and more choppy.

We were all pretty much in close proximity, then the undertow rocked our world. To be honest, I did not know the technical term, but as I was bobbing up and down, I noticed I was going out further and further. As I was bobbing, I noticed that I was unable to touch the sand as easily as before. It is at this point, either someone said something, or there was a very loud inner voice saying, "head back now!" Jimmy was closest to me, and we both began to struggle against the waves and the undertow; for me, I dove down to the bottom to feel the sand, and I began to use the sand to pull myself back to shore. I went a little ways and pushed up to grab some air quickly. I noticed others were struggling, trying to move forward. I said to myself; I gotta to get closer… I took a deep breath, went back down to the sand floor, and dug my hands down in the sand. At this point, I said to myself, "Open your eyes." I'll be damned if I die with my eyes closed. They initially burned, but adrenaline kicked in as I was pulling myself up; and as I was about to try to go back up for air, I felt a wooden column under the water. I said to myself it must be an old pier... then I felt another, and that's when I went back up for one last breath. I saw I was very close. Jimmy was flying, running on water to shore, Lance was with Paul, and they seemed to be moving further out with the waves. Lance, being a lifeguard, I figured he could handle it. What I found out later from Lance is pool skills are very different from ocean skills. Anyway, I hear someone telling one of the other guys to keep his head up and swim. Don't panic; everyone heard it, but we all were trying to get to the shore. I dove back down. I felt the old pier columns and used them to pull myself back to the shore. I banged my knee a couple of times on the columns, but you know, adrenaline kept me moving. Before I knew it, I could stand up and run onto the shore. I looked around; Jimmy was there. Lance, Paul, and Jerry were still out there. You can feel something terrible was about to happen. Lance barely got in, and he looked exhausted. Paul was still out there taking in water. Jerry was still out there, further and further away from shore; someone said, where is Jerry? As you looked out, we could see him struggling for his life, not able to move closer to the shore, due to the time of day. The lifeguards were heading out or had left. Someone ran to get them; we were watching the kid in the water, yelling at him to keep his head up; at that moment, I felt completely helpless, unable to provide any assistance or guidance. As we waited for help, I saw something that has stayed with me for over forty years. He held his head up and then went back down... he popped up quickly but went back down just as fast; he came back up slowly and then, disappeared. A bunch of lifeguards came up, "where is he?" He was right out there, straight ahead. They flew into the water. At that moment, time didn't stand; still, it changed. Seconds became minutes, and minutes became unbearable, full of anxiety. "Where's Lance?" He was on the shore. Paul miraculously got to shore, coughing and throwing up water; Jimmy is here. Veronica and Eric were like what happened? Are you ok? We seemed to be ok, but reality came back into view; lifeguards found him and came back to shore, but I wasn't sure what they came back with... it didn't look like someone that was with us— to the point of unrecognizable. He was bloated— they tried to resuscitate him. As they pumped his chest, water came out of his mouth. They did that for a while, and we knew, at that moment, one family's world will would be rocked to its core.

What was to be the start of a great weekend for returning college students and friends, became a moment in time that (for me) changed to disaster. I love the beach, and I love the water, but after that day, the next time I stepped on a beach was back in Virginia, and as soon as I touched the water, it felt like I was just punched in the gut. Visions of that day... seeing his body. I couldn't go any further than my ankle. It took a few years for me to move past that trauma. I haven't been out further than my waist since.

Looking back, I never realized all of the things that occurred that year, and how Lance has continued to persevere. Some folks may not want to hear this but check it out. Heaven and hell, good versus evil, are in us. We don't have to look up or down. We constantly battle ourselves, knowing what is right, or using our better judgment (that's God's fool), and instead, we want to go ahead and do our own thing. Damn the circumstances (that's Satan working on us satisfying our lust/ wants). If you spend time listening to Lance and the things he has and continues to accomplish, you can see God in him by the decisions he makes, and how he treats people. He's far from perfect, but the light he carries is a beacon for others. If they choose to look, now marinate on that.

- Brian Bookman

My brother has always been my hero! I remember the phone call that brought me to my knees, in tears, like it was yesterday. My mom answered the phone and started screaming, "No, no, no!" My dad had to take the phone to receive the worst news imaginable. My brother had been in a plane crash in Rhode Island. We were not given many details, other than Lance was alive. My dad mustered up all the strength that he could to take the lead and make plans. My dad informed my mom and I that we were going to drive to Rhode Island in the morning. I cried myself to sleep. The next morning, as we prepared to get ready, my dad had to hold my mom up in the shower, because she was so weak with grief.

The car ride seemed like it was forever, although it only took five hours.

There were several what-if questions from my mom and I during the ride. What if he dies? What if he has permanent damage? What if he

Can't play football anymore? My dad yelled, "stop it! My boy is going to be fine!" I tiptoed into Lance's hospital room in fear of the unknown. Sure enough, once I laid eyes on him, I screamed, because his face was black and blue and swollen, like a balloon. He had bandages everywhere, and his leg was in a cast. Lance made light of it by asking, "do I look that bad?" we all chuckled! From that point on, I felt confident that he would make a full recovery.

Not only did he defy the odds and make a full recovery, but within a couple of months, lance was back on a plane, two weeks after he got out of the hospital.

- Tracey Theobald

My friendship connection with Lance was instant from the first week of college, our freshman year. His personality was infectious. He was energetic, funny, positive, and completely comfortable in his own skin. He was unlike anyone I had ever met. There were too many great times and laughs to count, but my respect for Lance was really earned by watching him handle adversity with amazing strength and grace. Having a best friend who was of different gender and race, gave me a life perspective that I am forever grateful for. I learned a lot about friendship; that it's about unwavering support, trust, and loyalty. We kept a tight circle and provided each other with a soft place to land, if either of us had a struggle. These standards of friendship are what I've carried through life. Our friendship was not always understood by others, but we didn't care. You're going to hear about his challenges and how he reinvented himself multiple times. In my mind, his success in life came from his total authenticity, his work ethic, and his adaptability. He could pivot quickly, not just on the football field, but in life. He knew his strengths and weaknesses, and managed them accordingly, and was always true to himself. I have to say, out of all the college besties, I got the best one!

- Laurie Macpherson

This is John Skladany, recalling the recruitment of Lancelot Theobald Jr., and the plane crash while coming to the University of Maine for a football scholarship.

I was coaching football at the University of Maine, and one of my major responsibilities was the recruitment of student-athletes to come to the University. My recruiting area was Long Island, North and Central New Jersey. During the process of recruiting in that area, as I was involved with the high schools, I came across a running back by the name of Lance Theobald at Holy Cross High School. I got the opportunity to watch Lance practice and play in games as we evaluated the game film. I got a chance to visit with the coaches at his school, talk with the guidance counselor, and evaluate his transcript, and, at once, determined that he would be a viable candidate to come to the University of Maine to play football.

Watching him at practice and in the games, I could see a young man that had tremendous athletic ability. He was a running back with great balance, a really strong lower body, with legs, hamstrings, and quads that he could really run and run over people; he could also make cuts and outrun people. So, we thought he would be an excellent fit for our wing T offense at the University of Maine. As the recruiting process went further, and we got to visit Lance at his high school, we determined we'd like to get Lance to come for a visit to the campus at the University of Maine to see where he would like to go to school.

We also determined that we would like to give Lance a full scholarship, including his room, board, tuition, and fees. But with the visit, we were able to pay for the expense to get the young man to the university. And, coming from Long Island, we had Lance fly to the University of Maine. He had to take a flight from LaGuardia airport. I believe he was going to Providence, or Boston; I can't remember exactly, and then from Boston to Bangor. During the process of that, there was an incident. As his recruiting coach, I was going to pick him up at the airport and transport him to the University of Maine, where he'd meet the players, and we'd take him on his official visit, where he could see the campus, see our facilities, and see if it was a place that he would feel comfortable going to school.

I remember going to the airport to pick him up. And the plane arrived, I believe was from Boston, and he wasn't on it. So, I was wondering what had happened, if he had made the connection, and if there was a problem if he got on it in time. During the next few minutes, I was really contemplating what to do, and I checked on the airline, his original flight, and I found some horrifying news that the plane had crashed. And then I got on the phone and called his parents. At that time, we didn't really know anything, but we knew that the crash had happened, and we didn't know how serious, or if there were survivors, or exactly what it entailed.

Over the course of the next couple hours, we found out that Lance was okay, and he had done some heroic acts in helping some people to get off that plane. We heard that he had broken his foot and needed to put a pin in his foot, but that he was going to be okay. Well, as time went on, a few weeks went by, and I know he had had his procedure on his foot, and he was healing up, and we stayed in close contact. I asked if he would still be interested in coming to the University of Maine to take a visit and to see the campus and meet the players and the coaches and see all the facilities. He said yes. So, we went ahead and made the arrangements for him to fly up to the University of Maine up in Orono. And he had to fly into Bangor.

And I was a little skeptical myself. I wondered if the young man would be able to get on the plane and if his family would let him get on. But, lo and behold, his parents and Lance decided that the best thing to do was to get right back up on the horse and get to it. And he flew up to the University of Maine and got to see everything, got to meet everybody. We offered him a full scholarship that he accepted, and he ended up coming to the University of Maine. The things that drew me to him were not only his athletic ability on the football field and his academics in the classroom, but his personality. He was very outgoing, very confident, and self-assured. I thought he would have a chance to be a really successful college football player, get a degree and go on and really do something with his life and have a great future. And that all came to pass. Especially seeing that he had the courage, determination, and willpower to get on that plane again to come up to the University of Maine. I know he's had some other setbacks in his time as well, with some misfortune, but it just goes to show what type of character that young man has and the commitment he has to get things done. We're very, very proud of him.

As a running back at the University of Maine, he had an excellent career. I know he had a couple of tryouts in the national football league. Just goes to show what kind of ability he had. But we were really happy that he came to the University of Maine, to see him as a graduate of Maine and doing well as he is right now. It is not an easy task to undertake, to get your education, and to play division 1 football. There's a lot of time, energy, and physical exertion put into it. And it takes a lot of determination. And Lancelot Theobald Jr. certainly had that, and that's what drew me to him. I saw all those traits and qualities that would make a fine football player. And it really worked out well for him and for us.

- John Sklandy

I''ve known lance for more than fifteen years. We met in a tap dance class at American dance and drama studios. We both had a common goal to take tap classes with one of the greatest tap dancers in the world, Ted Levy.

Lance was extremely focused and dedicated to learning the skills that were taught. He was always on time for class—never missed a beat and was always supportive of other dancers. If you needed help with a step, he would help. I admired that about him, a man of integrity.

As I watched Lance each week in the tap class, I thought to myself; he is a good type for the theatre. I wondered if he could act. No sooner than I asked the question to myself, Lance announced that he was in an off-Broadway play. I saw him perform in this play as a detective interrogating a suspect. I was blown away! He approached the role with truth and believability.

I was so excited because I was the representative of a theatre company known as American Ensemble Theatre, which is now Open-End Repertory Theatre, founded by executive director Fred Sciaretta. We were in the process of casting, non-traditionally plays. One in particular: A Eugene O'Neil play, "Anna Christie". I was cast as the leading lady, Anna Christie, and we were looking for our leading man, Matt Burke. I found him the night I saw Lance in that off-Broadway play. The problem was Lance didn't know.

At first, I was afraid to ask him. I knew how busy he was. I pondered over my thoughts with Lois Simon, a good friend and a member of Open-End Repertory Theatre. She said, just ask him. I had already told Fred, our director, about Lance and that I wanted him to play Matt Burke. Fred suggested I ask Lance to just sit down and read a scene with me. I did that, and Lance got hooked. He loved the challenge of playing an Irishmen with a brogue accent. We then started our journey as cast mates, building a strong working relationship with each other and with a team of talented actors, along with our amazing director. We performed "Anna Christie", which was our first big production together. It was a hit! Lance carried on a role of an Irish seaman who falls in love with a woman on a barge. His honest work revealed the energy he put into playing his role as Matt Burke, and the effort to research his character and the play itself. We worked long hours into late evenings to get the play up and running.

Since then, Lance and I have performed many plays through Open End Repertory Theatre, and we did our first feature film, Eddie, directed by Fred Sciaretta, which debuted in 2021, on most major media platforms. Throughout the pandemic, we worked endless hours virtually on our most recent project, which is a trilogy about relationships, directed by Marc Theobald. We never stopped. We kept going, and we are still going.

Lance has been one of the best cast mates a person could ever have, with the greatest work ethic I have ever seen. He's professional, respectful, caring, conscientious, and shows up on time; he's willing to work long hours until the job is done, and he learns lines from a script with a quickness. He's one of the most lovable people in the world. I am so proud of him, and I am ever so grateful to have a friendship for life with my friend and cast mate, Sir Lancelot Theobald Jr.

- Angela Rostick

Lancelot Theobald Jr. Is a skilled teacher of tap and hip-hop. He has been a valued member of the faculty of the Berest dance center for over twelve years.

When Lance conducts class, he has a strong persona and demands discipline. He teaches work ethic. He teaches what it takes to learn to dance. Lance respects feelings when students are discouraged and talk about their reaction to having difficulty in class. They explore what attitude is necessary to improve. Lance talks about the process of learning and commitment. He talks about life skills. In other words, he is a life coach to his students, and in doing so, they connect with him. They listen with intent and reflection. He becomes a mentor. What better testimony than a letter written by a senior after many years of study, "lance changed my life."

Respectfully submitted.

- Olga Berest, owner and director of Berest Dance Center

After I graduated from Hampton University, I wanted to conquer the world. I just didn't know how I was going to do it. My cousin Lance had a tee shirt business, and I loved that he owned his own business. When Lance told me he was an exotic dancer and wanted me to be his assistant, I didn't understand what that meant. What does that have to do with tee shirts? Assist at what? What does a stripper need my assistance doing?? Do I keep my clothes on?

It wasn't until I saw the number of props lance used in his show, that I realized he needed an assistant badly. He had a chair, a rose, a night table, and a full-size futon. I felt like I was employed by u haul! Each prop had to be brought out to the dance floor at a precise music cue that Lance had rehearsed. It was a lot for a recent college grad that had never been in a club with 400 screaming, and sexually charged women before. I was horrible.

But I got to witness Lance's brilliance in dance. He didn't just take his clothes off. He was a former football player that danced with the grace of a ballerina. He took something that I looked at, just as a hobby, and made it an art form. He changed my view of exotic dance and art as a whole.

I followed Lance's lead into the arts and became a stand-up comic and television writer. It all started for me as Lance's assistant.

- Marc Theobald

When it comes to advancing as a tap dancer, there are plenty of people that talk about a good game, but Lance helps you make it happen. He has enabled me, coached me, and given me the confidence to attack any choreography. Throughout our journey together, he has been a true inspiration, not only as a mentor, but especially as a master of the process of how to transform a blank canvas into an outrageous piece of work, for the ears and eyes. His passion for tap dancing is what makes him a superior choreographer. While some may keep time (pun intended) and dismiss a class at the end of the hour as scheduled, lance's passion may take a lesson into overtime with joy, excitement, and insane energy! Lance is a true professional and holds his dancers to high standards while encouraging fun and creativity. My daughter and I feel blessed and honored to have Lance as our "tap dr."!

- Tali Tadmor

There are plenty of acquaintances in life but very few true friends. This sentence might sound like a cliché, yet it profoundly represents my life. Whether it was a word, a pat on the shoulder, or even a gesture, real friends left their footprints on every position change that defines who I am today.

Many Italians of my generation were fascinated with America and the American lifestyle. They marveled at anything made in the USA. Even the simplest of products were considered a hot commodity labeled as "Americano." Getting a hold of stuff like baseball caps and t-shirts was quite an achievement! So, one can imagine how incredibly cool it was playing American football in Italy back then.

Thanks to the NATO bases that were spread throughout the country after WWII, and efforts made by some trendsetters, the game started to be known and played among the Italian youth. Thanks to the support of NATO-based coaches and players, I was able to enjoy with others this amazing opportunity to play American football.

I would play for the "Oaks of Napoli." We began as a c league, and after a few years, we made it into the a1 league thanks to American NATO coaches and players. This was during Maradona's time, when Napoli's soccer team won the Italian championship, so when the Oak's Napoli team reached the A1 division, they were aspiring to find their own Maradona too. After recruiting & searching, the owners decided to hire a player from the greatest city in America, New York City. To us, it was a dream come true! Lancelot Theobald, a pro prospect running back, joined our team, and we were full of joyful excitement and enthusiasm.

Having someone as skilled as Lance on our team, encouraged me to focus on improving my skills as a defensive end player. I got a chance to go up against Lance during a training session doing the Oklahoma drill. We were use to training at sunset on a field surrounded by a jaw-dropping backdrop. The atmosphere was a stark contrast between the endurance such a sport demands, and the subtle beauty of the evening skies of Naples.

The Oklahoma style of playing demands that both the offensive player and defensive player lay down on their backs head-to-head. At the sound of the whistle, both players have to simultaneously jump onto their feet, followed by the runner breaking through the scrimmage line and the defensive player trying to tackle him.

I felt lucky to be the first team member to face Lance. I jumped to my feet at the sound of the whistle, determined to show the "Americano" that we were just as strong, but soon, I realized that the game was over and that his skills were beyond comparison. I still remember the humiliation of that head-to-head contact which forced me to retreat yards and yards back.

Nonetheless, there was something pleasant going on, with all that rush of adrenalin you only feel when you are face-to-face with a champion!

He astonished everyone with his power and strength. Like a real champion who's not after the glory, Lance shared his knowledge of the drills and techniques which he mastered during his career, to help improve our team skills, no matter what level they were at. That's when we realized that we had found our hero, true friend, and inspiration.

As Lance started playing on our team with squad number 34, we all understood that this guy, who wasn't much of a talker and often played double roles, whilst being heavily tugged from his shirt, which literally ended up torn after every game, was undeniably an example to follow. He proved to be an example, not only on the field, but in our daily lives as well. He never complained and was always generous and kind to his teammates. He never questioned a coach's choice or criticized a teammate who made a mistake. He was, by all means, a role model in words and deeds.

- Lucio Mucciariello

My name is Barbara, and I'm a middle-aged mom living in the suburbs of Long Island, NY. While seeking a fitness class more than 20 years ago, I stumbled upon a "dance with Lance" class at the JCC. Little did I know, choosing to take this exercise class changed my life for decades to follow. An unlikely collaboration developed between the fitness "teacher,"

Lancelot, and a group of middle-aged moms like myself taking that class. We formed a performing group that has since received international recognition. On the outside, we had very little in "common." But on the inside, however, many unseen similarities emerged. I discovered, like myself, Lancelot had a history of doing what was expected of him, but knowing he had dreams and passions that were quite different. When you hear Lancelot's story, you know that he made a brave decision to leave his career to become a performer, choreographer, and much more. Similarly, I spent decades in the medical profession, knowing that I had dreams and passions to perform, and over the age of forty, I changed lanes myself. Lancelot and I recognized the similarities between our journeys of discovering our true paths to inner happiness. On the outside, we looked different; we came from different types of neighborhoods, we were not the same age, and we had different religious belief systems, and yet, this shared drive to realize our dreams and passions later in life became the powerful basis for an amazing partnership/friendship.

Over the last two decades, Lancelot and I have developed and nurtured that performing group that has inspired people all over the world to try new things, even at an older age. We have raised countless amounts of money traveling and bringing our shared inspiration and motivation to fundraise for many worthy causes. During the lockdown of the 2020 pandemic, Lancelot and I were both isolated from our families. Simultaneously, the national news was focused on the George Floyd murder case, and it reminded Lancelot of his own trauma growing up in a neighborhood where discriminating behavior by the police and racial profiling were rampant and often affected him personally. When Lancelot shared with me that he was coping with feeling his past trauma, and lacking enthusiasm, we decided to put that "negative" energy into something very positive. We created the 'Push Up For Your Life' fundraising campaign, where Lancelot completed 10,000 pushups to raise money for the Equal Justice Initiative. Taking all our CDC precautions very seriously, we created a live video show of Lancelot doing these pushups and encouraged people to join us online; to turn all of these hardships into something meaningful. We raised over $10,000 in a short period of time, and even presented the organization with the big check, virtually! My friendship and business collaborations with Lancelot are the perfect, most beautiful example of how people with so many "outside" differences can be made up of the same hopes, dreams, passions, drive, humor, and intentions on the inside. We have made a lifelong friendship that will continue to inspire others, and of course, we will continue our good work raising awareness, raising funds, and entertaining people along the way. I will be the first one to read this wonderful book Lancelot has written with all the pride and awe of how one man can change the lives of so many people out of the decision to change his own.

- Barbara Adler

When Lance approached me to write a few words for his upcoming book, I was honored to oblige, because I have known Lance all my life. You see,

They Haven't Made An AX That Can Chop Down A Dream

Lance is my god brother. I have been there to see Lance grow from a child to the man that he is today, and all the milestones in between. There are so many qualities that Lance possesses that I could write about, but I will focus on Lance, the role model.

Lance is a very passionate person, and his passion leads him to be able to inspire others. When he decides to take on a cause, he throws himself into it wholeheartedly. When he played football, for example, he was always recognized for his passion and dedication to the team and to the game. His passion and dedication, in turn, inspired his teammates to give it their all. He wasn't the biggest player at the time, but he was the most dedicated and passionate player on his team. His actions show others what passion is and what passion does for yourself and for others.

Before I could talk about Lance in this role, I had to first ask myself, "what are the qualities of a positive role model?" My definition of a positive role model is one who possesses 1. Passion and the ability to inspire, 2. Clear set of values, 3. Commitment to community, 4. Selflessness, and 5. The ability to overcome obstacles.

Possessing these qualities is the main reason that I have asked for and had Lance appear on numerous occasions as a guest speaker at my school's career day events. As an educator who has been teaching in Brownsville, New York, for over thirty-three years, I know the importance of selecting a guest speaker who is a positive role model and a person with whom the students can respect and, more importantly, relate to. Lance is that person!

They Haven't Made An AX That Can Chop Down A Dream

My students were able to experience Lance's passion when engaging with them and answering their questions, questions that weren't "prepared" by the educators but were "their" questions to be asked. The students were able to have "real talk," as they described it. Not someone who is "Hollywood" but who came from "where they come from." A person who they could really look up to because he comes from where they come from, and he succeeded without being a hustler but one who is passionate and let his passions drive his success.

Lance is a fitness guru, an actor, and a dancer, all of which demonstrate that he lives by his values; "to live and be the very best that one can be." The students at my school have witnessed firsthand a "real" person live by his own code and be successful. As I always remind my students that "we must not just talk about it but be about it!" Lance continues to do just that.

Commitment to community is paramount to Lance. He is committed to his family, friends, and his professional community. As a role model, he is always other focused as opposed to self-focused, which enables Lance to give freely of his time and talents to benefit others. The students admired Lance for these qualities. He asked them about themselves and their goals instead of solely focusing on himself.

Related to the idea that role models show a commitment to their communities, the students at my school also admired Lance for his selflessness in giving up his time when they knew Lance had other commitments but canceled those commitments because he promised he would be their career guest once again.

Finally, the ability to overcome obstacles is one of the qualities that are essential for a positive role model to exhibit to be effective in showing people, especially students, that success is possible.

As I am sure, Lance will discuss how he had to reinvent himself to be successful. Not surprisingly, many of the students in my school appreciated that Lance had shared his amazing journey; they admire people who showed them that success is possible.

It was as Booker T. Washington once said, "success is to be measured not so much by the position that one has reached in life as by the obstacles which one has overcome."

As a result, I recommended to our graduation committee; Lance for the honored position of keynote speaker for our schools ----graduation exercise. With Lance participating in our school's career day as a guest/presenter and with the students always responding with such enthusiasm when he spoke, I knew that he would be the right person for the task at hand.

I suggested Lance because I needed an exceptional keynote speaker who was comfortable with himself and a person who could come across as having credibility and having both feet on the ground. I needed a speaker who could speak to the students like they were friends or family yet keep the students engaged.

The students hung on Lance's every word. He was charismatic, inspirational, funny, motivational, and relatable; he spoke with relevance.

Lance didn't have name recognition at the time, but he had the life experiences that the students had seen and perhaps had experienced themselves or knew someone who had also experienced setbacks. It was for this reason that I was so proud to have my god brother Lance come before them as the success story that he was. He knew how to turn his losses into successes, and these students would remember him and hopefully apply his skills to be triumphant themselves.

- Yvette Edwards

Made in the USA
Middletown, DE
03 January 2024

46918273R00149